Praise for *The Children of Roswell*:

"For many years I worked as a state and then federal investigator, assigned to criminal cases of the most horrendous crimes against children. There's a certain lost innocence that's often never regained when children are victimized or intimidated to keep silent. The story of *The Children of Roswell* is as tragic as it is shocking. We now know that the American government stooped to the lowest level of humanity by going so far as to issue death threats to child witnesses. This should inform the reader of two things: There was a *big* secret to be kept...and the secret keepers were willing to go to any lengths to *keep* it."

—Ben Hansen, lead host of Syfy Channel's *Fact or Faked; Paranormal Files*

"Up until recently my father, Jesse Marcel Jr., was one of the remaining eye witnesses to the Roswell event. He believed that everyone had the right to know the truth about what really happened in Roswell, July of 1947. Now that he has passed, I find that *The Children of Roswell* to be even more relevant since there are fewer and fewer firsthand account witnesses."

—Denise Marcel, daughter, Col./Dr. Jesse Marcel, Jr.

"The secrecy that shrouded the Roswell event has been passed down from one generation to the next. Schmitt and Carey have followed the story from the beginning of first contact through the sons and daughters and grandchildren who have heard about this mystery as part of an oral tradition determined to keep the truth alive, even when the gatekeepers deny it. This is an important book because it gives voice to those who have encountered the unknown and been treated badly by a government that knows better."

—Bryce Zabel, creator, producer, and director of *Dark Skies* and coauthor of *A.D. After Disclosure*

"The people most effected by what happened in the summer of 1947 have a voice through this book and not only are able to share the pertinent facts, but also the emotional impact this event continues to have on these people's lives. No credible judgement of what happened in the desert outside of Roswell so many years ago can be made without reviewing the testimonies recorded here."

—Alejandro Rojas, Open Minds Television, writer, Huffington Post

"The Children of Roswell conveys to the reader the trauma suffered by several generations in the wake of a very real and very dramatic event for a small, sleepy American town—or any town, for that matter."

—Yvonne Smith, C.Ht., abduction researcher, author, lecturer

"For millennia the red sands of the upland plains and valley side slopes of Chaves County were reworked by wind, then later gently pressed beneath the feet of the Jumanas Indians who called southeastern New Mexico home. Since the first week of July '47, few have toiled greater or combed more meticulously the aridic soil near Corona in search of truth than these authors. I was convinced the red sands of Chaves County would give up their secrets no more. Now I am hopeful *The Children of Roswell* may be our last best hope...for the truth."

—Richard Syrett, host, The Conspiracy Show

"Every time Schmitt and Carey write a new book on Roswell, we learn more about this fascinating mystery of the century. This time, through interviews with the child witnesses, we get astounding evidence of the event and the resultant government cover-up."

—Steven Jay Rubin, author, *Combat Films: American Realism 1945-2010*; *The James Bond Films: A Behind the Scenes History*

"With the *Children of Roswell*, Tom Carey and Donald Schmitt give us an opportunity to contemplate how the witnesses to Roswell have dealt with the trauma of being confronted with non-human intelligent beings and their technology. Perhaps even worse than trying to understand the significance of contact with alien beings is the fear these witnesses relive that was inflicted by government agents bent upon keeping the Secret of Roswell from the public at all costs. The threats were real; the trauma silenced them for years, until now."

—James E. Clarkson, Washington State Director, MUFON

"I found accounts of the first-hand testimonies by the Roswell residents to be compelling; and, the new information presented herein advances our understanding about what happened in 1947."

—David P. Hajjar, Ph.D. professor of Biochemistry and Pathology, Weill Cornell Medical College and Graduate School of Medical Sciences

"An apt and compelling follow up to *Witness to Roswell*. By covering the accounts and testimony of some of the key children involved in this case, the authors lay out a very persuasive and almost conclusive argument, that layers perfectly on top of their previous work."

—*Don Most,* actor, producer

"Never before has there been a book that reads like an old photograph. Every detail has the reader seeing in his mind's eye a time where excitement, dread, and curiosity gripped rural America. *The Children of Roswell* is like a readable scrapbook where the reader can imagine and even see the Roswell UFO crash in a fresh and remarkable tableau that never ceases to captivate historians and investigators alike. *The Children of Roswell* gives a fresh human approach where raw emotions were felt as witnesses tried to explain one of the most enigmatic moments in our history."

—Clyde Lewis, radio host and personality

"This is the most emotionally intimate and engaging research on Roswell ever published. Through the experiences, stories and bright eyes of *The Children of Roswell,* the authors provide powerful new insight into not only the undisputed facts, but also the overwhelming emotional impact on this closely knit community. Together with their prior work, the authors make it clear that it is the truth about Roswell which will allow both innocence and trust to return—not only to its children, but to each of us as well."

—Joseph G. Buchman, PhD, *www.josephbuchman.com*

Thomas J. Carey *and* **Donald R. Schmitt**

The Children

of

Roswell

A SEVEN-DECADE LEGACY OF FEAR, INTIMIDATION, AND COVER-UPS

 NEW PAGE BOOKS
A division of The Career Press, Inc.
Wayne, NJ

Unless otherwise noted, images are owned by the authors.

Images on page 88, page 97, page 108 from the 1947 Roswell Army Air Field (RAAF) yearbook.

Image on page 122 courtesy of Corbis/Special Collections, University of Texas at Arlington Library.

Image on page 126 is an Air Force photo.

Image on page 174 courtesy of James Clarkson.

Image on page 200 courtesy of Juanita Kaufmann.

The Children of Roswell

EDITED BY JODI BRANDON

TYPESET BY EILEEN MUNSON

Cover design by Brian Moore

Cover image by Konstantin L/shutterstock

Printed in the U.S.A.

To order this title, please call toll-free 1-800-CAREER-1 (NJ and Canada: 201-848-0310) to order using VISA or MasterCard, or for further information on books from Career Press.

The Career Press, Inc.

12 Parish Drive

Wayne, NJ 07470

www.careerpress.com

www.newpagebooks.com

Library of Congress Cataloging-in-Publication Data

CIP Data Available Upon Request.

In loving memory of
Julie Shuster and Jesse Marcel, Jr.,
two of the children of Roswell

— DRS

To my professor emeritus brother,
Frank,
who first got me interested in the subject
when we were teenagers, but, more importantly,
whose scholarly pursuits provided a younger brother
with a role model for life of the very highest order.

—TJC

Acknowledgments

*I*t is with true gratitude that we would like to acknowledge the following individuals for their ongoing assistance and support of our
work:

Dr. Kevin Randle continues to provide us with valuable oversight and independent information on the Roswell Incident. Stanton
Friedman, who opened the door for us to conduct our own independent investigation of the case, has been both critical and supportive.
Both have provided us with an experienced overview of wisdom
and insight. We have worked well together and look forward to
other mutual projects in the future. Anthony Bragalia has shown a
level of enthusiasm for Roswell that is only surpassed by our own.
He has assisted us many times in tracking down individuals as the
clock continues to run out for the WWII generation. His research
on advanced technologies influenced by the wreckage from the
1947 has also demonstrated a concerted effort by our government to
reverse-engineer the exotic materials.

Jack Rodden remains our main contact in Roswell and also
serves on the board of directors at the International UFO Museum
and Research Center. Jack and his wife, Mary, have always treated
us like family, and their warm hospitality through all these years is
much appreciated.

Speaking of the International UFO Museum and Research
Center, we are most proud of our association with the number-one

UFO museum in the world. Attracting visitors from more than 150 countries at the continuing rate of 200,000 people a year, anyone who is interested in this topic needs to see this facility to learn just how much the government is not telling them.

Many thanks to Karen Jaramillo, assistant director at the Roswell Museum, who is turning into our local investigator. We often call on her for pertinent information and background checks. She never disappoints.

Our good friend and colleague James Clarkson conducted the wonderful completion of the June Crain investigation, for which we are most grateful. This is how witness investigation is done.

It is with true respect and gratefulness that we acknowledge the support and encouragement of Congressman Merrill Cook and Senator Michael Gravel. After we lost Congressman Steven Schiff, their involvement is most welcome.

To Joe and Beverly Brazel, who continue to make their family namesake proud. We promise not to fail them.

For the wonderful generosity of Ben and Emma Loggins and Bart Sweeney, who have enabled us to continue our archaeological work at the 1947 debris field.

Dr. Joseph Buchman is a trusted confidant and provides much-needed counsel whenever asked. See you at the next dig, Joe.

Thank you to Jane Kilbourne for 30 years of devotion and all of her secretarial assistance.

A big thank-you to Bill Kilbourne for all of his technical help and keeping Don Schmitt's PC in top running order.

Fond wishes to our dear friends Gary and Sarah Holloway for their inspiring friendship and heartfelt support, and the use of their Segways.

The Roswell Historical Society for consistently serving as a photographic reservoir in documenting the participants of 1947.

A big thank-you to Hollywood producers Paul Davids, Bryce Zabel, Don Most, and Steve Rubin for believing in us and not giving up on us.

For the late Jeff Peronto, who secured for us all the video interviews of the Melvin E. Brown family in England. You are truly missed.

To all of the children of Roswell, please know that we are listening to you and making every effort to tell the world of your plight. This should have never happened in this country and it continues to demonstrate the extreme measures that were appropriated to secure the extreme.

Finally, to all of you, who continue to read our books, attend our lectures, and just root from the sidelines. We are forever indebted to you and hope to meet each and every one of you in the future and thank you personally. Keep holding on to your seat—as the Roswell adventure continues.

Contents

Foreword

*I*f you thought you knew everything there is to know about Roswell, think again! Roswell investigator/authors Donald Schmitt and Thomas Carey have meticulously peeled back a fresh, new layer from that hauntingly mysterious UFO and extraterrestrial (ET) event of nearly 70 years ago.

This is a book with stories told straight from the hearts and as seen through the eyes of children whose families and lifetimes have been shaped in unbelievably chilling ways so hard to imagine. Even though many of their parents who were there during or soon after this historic incident have now passed on, their children say they can never forget what they know and what they and their families had to do to survive it.

Now, they share the truth about what it was like to live behind closed doors in fear of government pressure because of "what they knew," the unsolved mysteries, the strange disappearance of the son of a key witness, a new clue about the mystery nurse reportedly involved in the aborted alien autopsy at the Roswell base hospital, other untold stories, and the gut-wrenching impact their families endured for decades that is still alive within them to this day.

As you read this special collection of emotional, heartfelt stories, you will learn how this historical incident, in some cases, tragically affected the children and families involved in this seven-decade documentation of fear, intimidation, and cover-ups. This book definitely delivers a powerful message through the personal trag-edies sprinkled with lighter moments as stories are recanted about typical teenagers reacting to the spaceship crash story that would forever change the little town of Roswell, New Mexico.

You'll learn why the children of Roswell feel compelled now to speak out about the lingering aftermath from what happened there nearly 70 years ago and why they feel it is critical the rest of us finally know about it.

Although this book is not only about one of the most famous UFO cases of all time, the chronology of events is important in connecting the dots to long-held, tightly guarded secrets as told to Schmitt and Carey in a masterful blend of true life stories of today and their historical past. These events, which took place within and nearby the town of Roswell in early July of 1947, have become an iconic connection between the topic of extraterrestrials and mil-lions of people worldwide. There are many reasons why this hap-pened, but one stands above the rest: The legitimate media did its job, as well as possible, under the circumstances at the time. How the media reported the story played a key role in shaping how the people involved directly were impacted, as you will see.

At noon on July 8, 1947, the intelligence office at the Roswell Army Air Field issued a press release announcing that a "crashed saucer" had been recovered, and a front-page article appeared in the evening edition of the *Roswell Daily Record*. The story was picked up by the wires, and articles appeared the next day in many news-papers around the world. It was, of course, a huge, mind-boggling story, and reporters were eagerly on their way to Roswell to cover it, interview witnesses, scrutinize and photograph spaceship crash evidence, and, in other words, do their job.

But they never got there. The commander of the Eighth Air Force, General Roger Ramey, certainly under orders from President Truman, conducted a press conference in Fort Worth, Texas, at 4 p.m. that same day changing the account to the recovery of a Rawin weather balloon. Reporters turned around, and interviews with the scores of witnesses did not take place. The "UFO cover-up" had informally begun. Had the president and the Army Air Force not reacted so quickly, news reporters would have arrived in Roswell, witnesses would have been interviewed, and evidence investigated, and the world may well have learned of the extraterrestrial presence among us in 1947.

To a journalist, it's always about what happened and why. This book underscores the bigger issue that the UFO/ET phenomenon is truly a significant part of a bigger picture of lies, deception, and deceit prevalent in our world today. People brave enough to challenge that are a vital part of the journalist's quest for answers in trying to figure that out. This takes us a big step further in that direction.

The Roswell story would reemerge when Major Jesse Marcel, Sr., the head of intelligence of the most famous unit in the U.S. military in 1947, came forward to researchers in 1978, and the rest is history. A small New Mexico town would become home to the world's most known incident related to the UFO phenomenon. You will learn how and why Jesse Marcel, Jr. became such a fighter for the truth, an "officer and a gentleman," and why he and his father both courageously came out from the closet of secrecy to challenge the official weather balloon storyline despite fears of government reprisal.

Despite two more explanations from the Air Force accounting for the Roswell incident, the extraterrestrial explanation remains standing on a platform built from interviews with hundreds of first and secondhand witnesses. Perhaps no pair of researchers has conducted more such in-depth interviews than Donald Schmitt and Thomas Carey. Their *Witness to Roswell: Unmasking the Government's Biggest Cover-Up* has now been eclipsed in *The Children of Roswell* in what legendary newsman Paul Harvey would call "the rest of the story."

Roswell, of course, is not the only evidence pointing to an extra-terrestrial explanation for the UFO phenomenon. Nearly 70 years of citizen science has amassed a mountain of such evidence. That being the case, why is the UFO question still not resolved? The vivid remembrances recounted by these family members may shed more bright light on that dark question.

Just when you think it can't get any more compelling, it does. An intriguing interview with NFL football great Tom Brookshier by Thomas Carey reveals a wide range of reactions as a teenager in Roswell in 1947 about what he witnessed and described as one of the strangest things he'd ever seen in his life, as well as his own run-in with a reporter about the "flying saucer."

Since that memorable 1947 summer, the American media and the United States government have been embraced in an elaborate dance around the most important revelation in all of human history. The media could report the UFO phenomenon, but it was not allowed to challenge the cover-up with imposing questions asked of authority. In *The Children of Roswell*, you will learn how the families were affected by that deafening silencing and media control. That media dance continues to this day, but the music has slowed and the tune is changing, because this story just won't go away.

Whatever agreements were reached in the late 1940s and early 1950s among the U.S. government, the television networks, and the big-city newspapers, that "understanding" regarding the UFO issue is eroding. It is only a matter of time before a major news venue challenges the status quo with the right questions asked of the right people, agencies, and services. It is the bravery of people like you will meet here, through their personal testimonies, that will help make that eventually happen.

As a broadcast journalist and veteran CNN news anchor with a lifelong curiosity about the UFO issue, I noted with interest how CNN engaged the phenomenon more frequently than any other network or cable news channels. Most of this coverage was aired on CNN's flagship *Larry King Show.* Over two and a half decades, King occasionally brought researchers and witnesses, including Jesse Marcel, Jr., on his program to discuss the UFO question, including the legendary October 1, 1994, show held just outside Area 51 in the Nevada desert.

Elsewhere, UFO-related documentaries are now ubiquitous on cable channels and usually get high ratings, as the interest to know what is going on in our universe continues to grow, not decline, through the years. Thousands of articles continue to be written in mainstream print and internet media, with photos and comments showing up more frequently on social media as well. Hollywood continues to draw from a seemingly inexhaustible list of extraterrestrial-related themes. However, the stories presented here are not Hollywood fiction but truthfully told, intimately revealed, and finally shared by those who have lived to tell how their lives and families were affected then, through the years, and to this day.

One day, world governments will likely acknowledge the truth behind the UFO phenomenon due to media pressure, a populist demand, collective evidence, and testimonies of thousands of witnesses from military pilots, high-level officials, and investigators to innocent bystanders, including the history being recorded here in this book. It would be the biggest news story of all time. *The Children of Roswell: A Seven-Decade Legacy of Fear, Intimidation, and Cover-Ups* may cause one to wonder: If the Roswell cover-up extended to the next generation, intimidating even the **children** of witnesses, what other vital information has our government withheld from all of us? It's an eye-opening, insightful must read for inquiring minds that will tug at your heartstrings!

Cheryll Jones

Broadcast journalist

Former CNN news anchor

. . . just the facts, Ma'am.

—Sergeant Joe Friday, Detective Division,
Los Angeles Police Department

Record enough facts, and the answer will fall to you like a ripe fruit.

—Franz Boaz, American anthropologist

Roswell in Perspective: The Human Response to an Extraordinary Event

Eyewitness testimony is in need of reinstitution of relevancy. It has been weakened by revisionists and cynics who establish a double standard for that which is accepted as fact. Facts are facts, and criminals are still being convicted by the sole declarations of very human witnesses. Ufology has always and should always require a much higher scientific standard of acceptance due to the possible extraordinary nature of the phenomenon. Skeptics withstanding, those of us who still profess objectivity should allow witnesses every opportunity to profess the facts as they know them even when we don't like what they're saying, lest we become nothing more than story gatherers and fall into the same complacency trap as most contemporary journalists find themselves on the subject of UFOs.

For these past 25 years a most concerted effort has been raged to find a resolution to the one of the most perplexing and unflappable mysteries of all time—that apparently insurmountable question that has seen all of us grow older without any victory in hand: What actually did fall out of the sky outside of Roswell in 1947? The government has tossed out possible explanations, like platitudes coming from a 5-year-old, investigators have debated not if, but where and even still how many, and debunkers continue the damage control, all to no avail. After putting many years into eliminating every alternative explanation, only two possible scenarios remain: The Roswell Incident perpetuates a grand campaign to cover-up some super-secret project gone awry—or it really *did* happen as all the witnesses contend that it did. It is amusing how many of us subjectively dismiss hundreds of eyewitness accounts and simply insert a random hypothesis, then seek to make all the known facts magically fit the new pair of shoes (the "theory of the month," as we like to call them). Such would prefer that someone egregiously fabricated the entire affair to cloak the truth with the proviso that someday, hopefully in our lifetime, a more open government will release the files and the true nature will come spewing forth. Unfortunately, officialdom keeps fumbling around in the dark and has actually created more suspicion then solution—all in a rather nondescript fashion. Apparently, this has always been for effect and not public awareness. Control of outgoing information is still the primary precept of the government. Often, its own fears and ignorance of the facts are its most motivating emotion.

With disclosure *not* at hand, UFO research—and specifically the 1947 Roswell event—has arrived at a juncture of public consciousness and acceptance as to the true nature of what lies behind the legend, the myth of what started this all. With this pretext, readers are asked to don their best detective caps and reexamine the origins of the plot. Without prejudice or bias, we will ignore every detailed nuance and focus on the human aspect in the entire Roswell syntax. For this introduction most names have been omitted to focus on earthly tendencies. We have published, end-noted, and referenced the entire embodiment of sources for more than 20 years. Most is on the public record. Reinvestigating the manner of response of those involved will demonstrate the full scope of this now-iconic case. We shall attempt to separate the "story" from what the eyewitnesses' state and swear as fact. We will reexamine Roswell through the eyes of the novice and see where human perspective begins and a jaundice eye intervenes—where official position is countered by eyewitness position. We shall conduct a pragmatic investigation of the case from start to finish and observe if the human behavior matches expectations of something mundane or truly something extraordinary. And lastly, we will examine the immediate aftermath and whether the actions of the authorities coincide with the behavior of those who have just buried the Roswell saucer. Was it really "case closed," as the Air Force continues to dismiss the incident even today?

We begin with the hot, lazy summer of post–WWII in 1947. The "flying saucers" officially arrived the last week of June and became instant celebrities on all news fronts. Mass hysteria was not the issue; clearly someone else's "hardware" was invading our airspace. Never to miss an opportunity, advertisers and pranksters jumped on the bandwagon and attempted a number of publicity stunts and isolated hoaxes. All were easily identified, but people anxiously continued to peer at the skies. For the military this was no laughing matter. With each passing day of failure to identify the intruders, the Pentagon was pressed for answers from both the White House and the general public. Witnesses were both seeing and photographing aircraft that outmaneuvered, outperformed, and outflew anything scrambled after them. A nervous tension started to replace amusement as military officials provided no explanations. Now, in the face of such a situation, how should we expect an average, sophisticated, non-superstitious population to react? For those who have suggested that the entire country was caught up by a haunting reminder of the not-forgotten broadcast of *War of the Worlds,* history proves otherwise. According to major newspapers at that time, survey choices, which included everything from U.S. military secret devices to foreign spy planes, a mere 2 percent of those polled actually thought we faced a possible intelligence from off the planet—hardly the numbers that would support the final conclusions of those who peacefully resided in and around Roswell, New Mexico, in July 1947. As a matter of fact, many of the key witnesses directly linked to the event, never heard the famous radio broadcast before that time. Nevertheless, not one of them anticipated the life-altering events yet to come.

According to the Air Force's Project Blue Book there were more UFO sightings at that time in New Mexico than anywhere else in the nation. The Land of Enchantment was clearly the subject of someone's curiosity. Russian spy planes? Top Secret atomic testing? Whoever was behind the growing dilemma, New Mexico was tracking unknowns at a growing intensity, and America already had the [atomic] bomb. "We didn't need any more excitement than that," as one officer put it.[1]

The vast portion of high desert in the central part of the state is open grazing land. Ranchers were more than casual bystanders for the constant demonstration of military showmanship. So when these civilians reported hearing an explosion amidst thunderclaps the night of July 2nd, the late hour alone was pause for their curiosity.

This concern bore fruit the very next dawn. Ranch foreman W.W. "Mack" Brazel routinely rode out to inspect the previous rainfall, and that morning he stumbled upon a scene that would forever change his life. We know that Brazel had no knowledge of all the saucer excitement spreading throughout the country, so he obviously didn't race to that proposition. Did the cowboy conduct himself as he had for all the typical unexpected "debris from the sky" of the past? Being a responsible supervisor, he normally would have gathered up this "garbage" and kept it out of the grazing path of the cattle and sheep. Present-day evidence of this was an over-flowing water tank brimming with weather balloons, for many years at the main ranch house up until around 1992. Ranchers continued to deposit such refuse in this receptacle for more than 50 years. But Brazel didn't just gather this material and dispose of it as he should have. Later, he would lament the extra effort of having to circle the sheep 2 *miles* around this pasture, clearly suggesting the extent of the debris. He stated the sheep were afraid of the strange material.

What transpired next was also not consistent with the ordinary. The perplexed rancher took samples of the wreckage to his neighbors, asking for help. Next, he went into the nearest town of Corona and placed a call to his boss in Texas—still seeking answers. Pieces from the crash started to circulate around town including the local pub, which left the patrons just as puzzled as Brazel. Artifacts even stole the show at the annual Fourth of July Rodeo in Capitan, an hour south of the debris field. From all accounts no one could cut, burn, or identify this unusual material. That same evening a frustrated Brazel returned to the debris field to drag a large section of the "unknown" wreckage to a livestock shed 3 miles away. Such would be all of the activity of civilians and their response to an extraordinary event, and night would come the first day.

Word was spreading quickly throughout the surrounding region, and with it souvenir hunters made their way to the scene of all the speculation. This was hardly the behavior of hardworking, no-nonsense, salt-of-the-earth individuals whose handshake was their bond and who disliked being crossed even more. They weren't being fooled about this; they needed to see for themselves. As described, by man, woman, and "child," the rumors were true, and they grabbed the most exotic pieces as in some unattended candy store. Take note: Neighbors hid their bounty in caves, in water tanks, under floor boards, in sacks of feed, in fruit sellers, and even inside jars of canned peaches. Two obvious questions are: Who were they hiding this evidence from, and why did they treat it so secretively? Nevertheless, for something so sensitive and important to 'someone's' national security, no authorities—we repeat, no one— was looking for anything. Nothing was reported missing. Such was the continuing civilian response to this extraordinary event.

Still, not having a single answer, Brazel attempted one final resolution. After completing his end-of-the-week chores, he headed for Roswell to finally report it to the authorities there. Not even a Lincoln

County state police officer who was supposed to know everything that was going on in his jurisdiction could recognize the wreckage. Up to that point not a single individual recognized a conventional piece of material.

Unfortunately for Brazel, neither the sheriff nor any of his deputies could offer any help. Nonetheless, the sheriff was so impressed with the box of scraps sitting on his desk that he dispatched two of his deputies to head north and check out the story. Nevertheless, Brazel was still batting a big zero.

What happened next created the very nightmare scenario that officialdom fears most: The press, albeit serendipitously, got wind of the growing mystery. Radio station KGFL talked to the rancher over the phone while he was still at the Chaves County Courthouse. Brazel not only charged that someone was responsible for cleaning up all that wreckage but next splashed gasoline on an already-smoldering fire. "They weren't human," he proclaimed. The reporter, in stunned disbelief, still urged the distraught man to contact the Army at the Roswell Army Air Field (RAAF). This sounded like something they would need to know about immediately.

Keep in mind that this was the Sunday of a Fourth of July weekend. Now imagine that whatever story some old rancher was selling, not only the head of intelligence of the most elite military unit in the United States, the 509th Atomic Bomb Wing, takes immediate note and also the very commanding officer of that very base unit gets involved. You can stop imagining. The mystery deepens as the base commander can't identify the debris either, and there is absolutely no report of any downed aircraft, secret tests, or rocket launches. If anything happened around Roswell, they would have been the first notified. And for that matter, the RAAF was always on alert—with the bomb and its security. Whatever this material was, and wherever all the rest of it was, it sure got the senior officer's attention. Why else should he dispatch his very head of intelligence plus the equivalent of foreign intelligence? The latter in the event it was something manufactured in another country. Why else was the head of CIC (Counter Intelligence Corps) sent? And if that wasn't enough concern, with a box of the true wreckage in hand, why did he immediately go up the chain of command and alert his boss in Fort Worth? And if that doesn't suggest the seriousness of the situation, why does his boss immediately contact his boss in Washington? Clearly, these high-ranking military officers found themselves in the same state of disorder as the rancher. Lastly, the Pentagon wanted to see firsthand and quickly ordered some of the material flown east to its attention. The growing interest in the unusual material had now advanced all the way to Washington. Total ignorance remained the prevailing situation. Brazel and the two officers arrived back at the ranch running out of daylight; it was then in the hands of the military.

Sunrise found the two officers anxiously perusing the then-ransacked arroyo, as wreckage had scattered with the prevailing wind. Brazel just hoped for this to all end and to get back to running the spread. The army wanted this to be one of ours in the worst way.[2] But there was so much of the crash remains and it extended for almost a mile. Quickly, they determined that it was a mid-air explosion that caused it to rain the components in a fan-shape pattern. There was much more than they could load into two vehicles. And just as the samples they had handled back in Roswell, the field was strewn with identical material. They proceeded to gather and contain all that they could while Brazel returned to his duties.

Back in Roswell, the press was getting antsy. What if the story about the crash of the flying saucer was true? They had to find the rancher, get his name from the sheriff, and grab him for the exclusive of the century. Radio station KGFL conspired behind military backs to undercut their authority. Freedom of the press would not be stifled. It would take the better part of the day to find the target of their abduction plans. Brazel would spend the night at the radio station and on a wire recorder to talk about "little men." Not far from there, the returning intelligence officer roused his wife and 11-year-old son to share with them an experience none would ever forget (I-beams with strange symbology) and talk about material not manufactured on this earth. Washington remained watchful late into the evening but night still fell the fourth day.

The very next morning, while Brazel sipped a cup of coffee in the kitchen of the majority owner of radio station KGFL, the RAAF base commander assembled his senior officers for an extra-early staff meeting to access the escalating situation. But before his two intelligence officers would even make their report of the debris field 65 miles northwest of town, there had been a new development just 40 miles to the north: the remains of a small ship and additional bodies. And if that wasn't disconcerting enough, the sheriff, fire department, press, and other civilians were already at that scene. The situation could have gotten completely out of hand, but the colonel was relieved to report that the entire area had been cordoned off, roads blocked, and witnesses warned not to talk.

Subterfuge is a military specialty, and Washington already had Roswell material in hand for two days. No knee-jerk reaction here. They had to admit something, but cooler heads chose the old scarecrow technique: First, build it up. Then, tear it down. The press release was all but carefully written. Timing was crucial. The later it hit the wires, the less chance it would make all the afternoon paper editions—and none on the East Coast. It was quite masterful. The base commander's boss was ready to fly back to Fort Worth to put phase two into effect. Within a matter of hours the slow evolution from saucer to weather balloon would begin. All this while mechanical engineers at Hangar P-3 pounded on a larger piece of the real wreckage with a 16-pound sledge hammer. "Still no dent," as one of them remarked. Washington would support the initial press bulletins. They had just this one opportunity to make it work, and so the cover-up went into a full court press. Meanwhile, back at the ranch...

Fifty to 60 men descended on the sleepy, open range with a mission of recovery and cleanup. Their orders were as follows: If it doesn't move, pick it up. Shoulder-to-shoulder they marched with burlap sacks on hands and knees in the 100-degree desert sun. They deposited the artifacts in wheelbarrows that were then rolled to checkpoints where each remnant was tagged and numbered. Lastly, trucks were loaded with wooden crates and headed back to the base in Roswell—only to return for another load and another. "Looks like you had a crash here," the local mortician commented back in town.

The situation 40 miles north of Roswell was much more urgent. Heavier equipment was required, including a flatbed, and security resembled an incident of utmost national security. Most involved with the recovery operation were not allowed within specific perimeters. Outside personnel, specialists including engineers, and crash investigators were called to the scene. Photographers were recording every move of the operation and when the ambulance trucks arrived. The RAAF base commander conveniently announced his leave departure after the press release went out. In reality, his vacation amounted to a picturesque tour of high desert plains overseeing the entire retrieval. The Army Field Manual provided no mention of such a strategic project. This was all uncharted territory.

An immediate search for Mack Brazel ensued and fortunately for the authorities they located him in short order. The wire recording was also appropriated, in total defiance of the First Amendment. From beginning to end, the law didn't apply in this entire affair. Reaction and response took on unprecedented proportions. And the most extreme behavior was yet to be applied. The main focus was to confiscate and contain every last piece of physical evidence still unaccounted for. People's rights were secondary. People were simply obstacles. And the evidence didn't cooperate; it provided no answers. No serial numbers or return-instruction tags were ever found.

Personnel at Roswell were excluded at every opportunity. Outside officers, MPs, photographers, even doctors and nurses arrived from parts unknown to take over the entire campaign—more eyewitnesses to offer professional opinions and assess the situation. "Something big had clearly happened."[3] But no one was talking. Men were called in to perform specific duties from individual units. Most were piecemealed to prevent talking after all the dust would hopefully clear. Emotions were cast aside, and alcohol helped as they performed like machines set on overdrive. Time was their enemy as the assigned floundered for unyielding solutions.

Further attention had to be diverted from Roswell. Only the intelligence officer was specifically named in the press release and he was being sent to "higher headquarters." The base commander took a holiday *after* the holiday weekend, and then the rancher who started the whole commotion was nowhere to be found. It was all so contrived. And next, the press had to be shut down. Calls came from Washington from the FCC with threats to sanction media outlets within 24 hours. Warnings to the Roswell press came all the way from the FCC in Washington and executive secretary T.J. Slowie. One of the U.S. senators from New Mexico followed up with the obligatory, hand-wringing call about it being "out of his hands."

On a grander scale, the FBI intercepted a national wire transmission attempting to report the true nature of the incident, stopping it dead in its tracks. A news blackout was in effect until a new story could be substituted. The process was in the works but synchronization was crucial. A scapegoat was also needed. The stage was being set for the press conference of the century in Texas. Would the U.S. government unveil for the entire world the actual wreckage brought in by the anonymous rancher as well as by the two intelligence officers, or, after high-level scrutiny, the same material sent to Washington *two days* before? They've now had as much time to rewrite one of the biggest stories of all time. All the chosen actors just needed to stick to the script—all while the rancher was being harshly interrogated back in Roswell. No customary phone calls were allowed to family or legal counsel. With no arrest, due process was not mandatory. The military had no authority over the civilian, which made the full-body search he experienced all the more undignified.

Unbeknown to the head of the 509th intelligence office, disguised packages were being loaded into the cargo haul of the waiting B-29 *Dave's Dream*. Originally the final destination was to have been Wright Field in Dayton, Ohio, but this special shipment, wrapped in brown paper, was intended for display at the late afternoon press conference in Fort Worth. And the general wanted the main actor to be there to take his bows. A change of scenery was about to take place. There, strewn over the general's floor, was a clump of rotting Neoprene rubber, wooden sticks, *blank* masking tape, string, and one-sided reflective foil. One lone reporter allowed into the officer's room would comment about the strong rubber stench. The Intelligence officer from Roswell was ordered to pose for two awkward photos, and then instructed to exit the stage and keep his mouth shut. Proclaiming there was no longer any need for such common elements being examined in Dayton, the general had just canceled the show. The curtain was about to come down. Discreetly, the real material went on to Ohio. The FBI's Dallas office confirmed that.

Meanwhile, in Roswell, reality proceeded in high gear. Wreckage continued to be trucked onto the base, the relatively intact craft of unknown origin arrived on a flatbed through the east gate, and the biological remains were examined under the strictest security at the military hospital. Everyone was working on pure adrenalin, and human emotion got the better of some. Fear was put aside by a call to arms, but this was never anticipated in anyone's army. Personnel followed orders under the premise that someone actually knew what was going on.

But ignorance prevailed. All they could do was stall for time while containing the occurrence, even if it should take years. A tent was set up within a new chain-link fence on the far southwest end of the tarmac. Guards were posted at the unusual location which was right next to the garbage incinerator. Someone commented that it was the perfect place to disguise an unknown odor. Rotting rubber it was not. Nervous eyes glanced skyward as night fell at the end of the the fifth day.

A relief detail arrived at the refuse site at dawn, but everything had been cleared out: The tent, its contents, and the metal fence were all gone. The only evidence left behind was a set of large airplane tracks in the dewy grass where something unknown had been secured overnight. Strange.

That same morning the weather balloon explanation served as a banner headline throughout the nation. The press bought the retraction and the public was relieved. The same military that had just won the war had once again prevailed, and now the normal rituals of summer could return. But even for the first atomic bomb wing in the world, nothing in their training seemed to apply to the mission still at hand. And with the balloon story taking effect, the "loose lips" policy took precedence. That part they lived every day.

As more of the remaining evidence was hurriedly transported from Roswell, additional troops were dispatched to finalize the cleanup at multiple sites north of town. Every last piece of debris needed to be secured; that also included the pieces that fell into civilian hands. So while the MPs were collecting every trace of the paper trail within the local media outlets, others were pulling up floorboards, dumping over water tanks, slitting open sacks of feed, and sampling the canned peaches while ranch families could only watch in total bewilderment. And no one had heard from or had seen the rancher for days.

The White House resembled a war room, as unscheduled meetings continued to express the utmost concern for what had fallen out of the sky in New Mexico. The deputy Army Air Forces chief sat through meetings with the Secretary of War, the head of the Armed Forces Special Weapons Project, the chair of the Joint Chiefs, and the president. Multiple meetings that overlapped and interrupted each other transpired for the entire day. It would appear they didn't get the weather balloon memo. Two secret service emissaries were dispatched to oversee the recovery operation and report directly to the commander-in-chief. Familiar faces had to remain in the shadows. The public had to accept the conventional—but all actions from those directly involved continued to suggest otherwise.

Mack Brazel was ready to denounce the incident within a few days of being taken into custody by the Army. His retractions to the press began on Wednesday, July 9th. Friends of the rancher and others witnessed military officers escort their next pawn to the main newspaper and the two radio stations. The recantation was that of simply misreporting an obvious weather balloon. Next time, Brazel wouldn't say a word, "If I find anything besides a bomb...."[4] Undoubtedly, the main reason for the civilian's detention served a greater purpose than the meager retraction of his story. Brazel had seen much more, and they had to enlist him as an apparent willing member of the sideshow. More to the point....sixty-nine years later his haunting remark resounds louder than ever, "They weren't green."[5] Another unscheduled flight later that afternoon would suggest the validity of that remark as testified by all who witnessed it. What had been secured the night before inside the temporary tent was now in a guarded crate loaded into a B-29 named the *Straight Flush* at atomic bomb pit Number 1. Almost 24 hours after the general had "emptied the Roswell Saucer," he, other officers, and a mortician eagerly awaited the arrival of additional remains contained within that large wooden box. The irony of "wooden" crash dummies is too good to pass up.

The recovery operation was quickly winding down on all fronts and Roswell townspeople were persuaded to put the entire incident behind them.

But the tentacled reach of the U.S. government was about to take aggressive action: confiscation of media reports, oaths of secrecy to military personnel, commissioning both elected and civil officials to perform proxy deeds of suppression and intimidation, plus the most heinous violation of the U.S. Constitution: the use of the military to physically threaten with death the very lives of its citizenry. Military search teams would continue to recover remnants for years after the story was buried, and Brazel's own son had material retrieved by the military *two years* after the incident. One need only examine the aftermath of specifically Mack Brazel. According to all sources, the humble cowboy was robbed of his very spirit. Family members stated that the incident "destroyed" the sheriff who would not run for reelection, and the RAAF public information officer, destined to go all the way to general rank, resigned. So did the intelligence officer, who in the aftermath of Roswell, is known mainly for two posed photographs with balloon wreckage. Others were immediately transferred and others promoted for being good soldiers. No one was reprimanded. No one was demoted. The RAAF base commander went on to Washington and got his four stars. Civilians were clearly the victims of the harshest of treatment, all to insure their full cooperation.

The military is a dictatorship, whereas civilians have rights guaranteed by our forefathers. The Chaves County Courthouse in Roswell, being surrounded by MPs, and the metal-like pieces, originally brought in by the rancher and then hidden by the sheriff, physically recovered as his daughters watched in horror, demonstrates the crux of this entire historic event: It all revolved around the physical evidence. Any remnants of a secret test, no matter how controversial, are still prosaic in nature. No matter how exotic, in the year 2016, no one has yet to develop near-indestructible, paper-thin material that has perfect memory.

The constant talk in a growing number of deathbed testimonies about "little men" and "little people" isn't about short-statured humans or shaved monkeys, as some skeptics have proffered. All of the witnesses have been very clear about this. Last confessions are admissible in American courts for a reason, and if we throw out the ones we don't like we have to toss out all of them. Roswell should be no exception.

As a collective sigh of relief fell over America, and the rest of world for that matter, New Mexico had just experienced a full scorched-earth policy that left its residents bitter and angry at the very people who were entrusted with their safety and well-being. The very relationship between the RAAF and local Roswellians was forever strained. A dark cloud enveloped the entire situation, but the Pentagon was far from finished with its damage control. Damn all the flying saucer reports and the people who see them.

The next page, in the Army's newly written handbook, was a nationwide attempt to dismiss *all* flying disk sightings. It was reasoned that if the balloon explanation could explain away actual physical evidence at Roswell, how much simpler it would be to provide a long-standing solution for the entire phenomenon. As a result, balloon launch demonstrations were publicly conducted at military facilities across the country. From New York to California, witnesses saw firsthand that a balloon, with an attached radar kite at 10,000 feet, could easily be construed as something unordinary. The irony was that the very same weather device that burst the balloon at Roswell, next served to deflate the entire saucer mystery. No one in the media ever noted how anyone could possibly misidentify a weather balloon on the ground right in front of you.

While this public charade was taking place, the very officer who would later be called the Air Force's "saucer man" was hitting the airwaves and mocking the very people who would even see such things. During an El Paso radio interview the general was asked about the wave of sightings throughout the entire nation. He responded that yes, it was true that there had been reports throughout every state in the country, "except Kansas, which is a dry state."[6] The UFO ridicule factor was officially born.

Upstairs[7], the government remained in a frantic state of confusion as it stalled for time in seeking out answers from a heap of crumbled wreckage and visitors literally out of this world. Experts in their respective fields were immediately dispatched to rewrite scientific history as they knew it, with hopes that the sun would still rise in the east the next morning. For example, renowned meteorite expert, Dr. Lincoln La Paz, arrived in Roswell within a few weeks after the incident with orders from Washington. Assignment: Determine the *speed and trajectory* of the crashed craft of unknown origin. (Note to reader: Balloon crashes are not gauged by either measurement.) Aside from T-2, which would become the Foreign Technology Division at Wright Field, metallurgists and engineers were enlisted from the Bureau of Standards, General Electric, Rand Corporation, and Hughes Aircraft. Just down the road in Columbus, Ohio, Battelle National Laboratories was contracted by Wright-Patterson to conduct developmental research on "self-healing" metal.

Air Intelligence in Washington sought its own resolutions, so it urgently requested a report from the Air Material Command (AMC) at Wright Field under the command of Lieutenant General Nathan F. Twining. The Pentagon wanted to get to the bottom of the entire "flying disk" affair. Just two months after the Roswell physical evidence was transported to Dayton, Ohio, Lieutenant General Twining held a secret conference with personnel from the Air Institute of Technology, Intelligence from T-2 (Foreign Technology Division), the Office of Chief Engineering Division, and the Aircraft, Power Plant and Propeller Laboratories of Engineering, Division T-3. If the general was attempting to corroborate "hardware," he couldn't have gone to better consultants. Clearly, these were "nuts and bolts" experts, not simply lights-in-the-sky speculators. Combined with what Twining knew firsthand to be the truth about the recovery at Roswell and whatever late-breaking status reports he gleamed from these consultants, he decided how to the respond to the original demand.

On September 23, 1947, Twining signed a secret memorandum, which, after approval from the Pentagon, was sent to Brigadier General George Schulgen, chief of the Air Intelligence Requirements Division (AIRD). The memorandum stated that the phenomenon was real.

Pursuant to the Pentagon's ongoing effort to ascertain the full scope of the situation, AIRD sent out a Draft of Collection Memorandum on October 28, 1947. The Pentagon was attempting to "collect" specific information from all intelligence sources from outside the United States, including England, France, Sweden, Finland, USSR, Turkey, Greece, Iran, China, Norway, the Philippines, and commanders-in-chief at other U.S. facilities around the world. The document was a further attempt to gather technical insights to what had crashed just a few months before in New Mexico. This final process of prosaic elimination cited "Unusual fabrication methods to achieve extreme light weight and structural stability," as well as "The presence of an unconventional or unusual type of propulsion system...."[8] Some of the actual replies have never been disclosed.

On December 30, 1947, Major General Lawrence C. Craige, director of Research and Development in Washington, issued an order establishing the first official U.S. government UFO investigation.

Code name: Project Sign (Project Saucer). And on January 22, 1948, Project Sign officially initiated work as a branch of Air Technical Intelligence Center (ATIC) and was headquartered at Wright-Patterson, where, six months before, all the physical evidence from Roswell had arrived. And it was without any surprise that the newly formed project was given a 2A priority (1A being the highest in the Air Force). It should also be emphasized that the very top people at ATIC were assigned to the project with the intent of providing the answers that physical evidence alone failed to yield. The rest, as they say, is history. One need not point out that this entire full-scale response was over a mere weather balloon device—or so they say.

This should remind all of us of the great tragedy of Roswell and the human element in dealing with something potentially inexplicable. No other explanation can demonstrate this depth of earthly emotion and transcend it for a lifetime, only to have it diminished time and time again by forces intent on suppressing the actual facts.

What remains even more disturbing is the manner in which innocent bystanders to affairs managed by adults are targeted with the same strong-arm measures enforced on their elders. Who speaks for the many families who survived the aftermath of 1947, those forced to live in silence by inexorable foes? Their nightmares originated not with invaders from space, but rather with the phantom caller, the stranger on the street, the car that keeps following. Inasmuch as it has been demonstrated that all the adults, whether military or civilian, independently responded in the same manner to the unprecedented events at Roswell, likewise the children reflected that same concern. But the children became the exception to the rule, as children are defenseless and grow up relying on those same adults for protection and security. The extreme measures enlisted to prevent the truth from becoming reality, destroyed that. Children became pawns to buttress the same threats implemented to coerce the adults into total compliance. The children of Roswell paid the ultimate price, compelled to abandon their country's guarantee to keep them safe from the monsters in the closets. Since 1947, agents of that same government have long hid in those closets—often acting the monsters.

In the first uncensored edition of his book, *Report on Unidentified Flying Objects* (1956), former Project Blue Book director Captain Edward Ruppelt stated, "By the end of July [1947] the UFO security lid was down tight. The few members of the press who did inquire about what the Air Force was doing got the same treatment that you would get today if you inquired about the number of thermonuclear weapons stockpiled in the U.S. atomic arsenal. At [ATIC there was] confusion to the point of panic." What an amazing admission. What could have possibly caused that "panic"? The invaders from space had just been sent packing in their weather balloon in New Mexico. Eyewitnesses who knew otherwise were all contained and had no proof to challenge the secret-keepers. Recall that wonderful scene in the Showtime made-for-TV movie *Roswell* in which the oversight committee is brainstorming the aftermath of the incident. The military general bemoans the dire situation: "We're supposed to insure domestic tranquility, not eliminate it. What if the people think we are not in control of the skies!?" The Secretary of War very stoically replies, "They'd be right."

Secrets become the responsibility of those entrusted with their disposition. After almost 70 years, the final truth remains in *their* hands. Our job remains: to break it free. For if all the witnesses are somehow wrong, it changes nothing. But if they are right—any one of them—it changes just about everything. The dead continue to cry out the truth, and governments seldom proclaim truisms unless it advances their cause. To concede such an event and take responsibility for the multitude of constitutional violations to American citizenry, including to children, who have decried the extreme malfeasance undertaken to conceal and bully them into silence, will never happen. For us to misconstrue the hidden agenda of the keepers of the Holy Grail besmirches those who have bravely stepped forward and opposed them. History is compiled of testimonies and personal accounts of people such as these. It is time we end revising their information to fulfill our own motives and those of malevolent intent. Inasmuch as we would like to dismiss any notion that they speak of a solution from off the planet, we do have to concede that their pattern of fear and intimidation from forces unknown makes their plight no less disconcerting. For too many of the children of Roswell this has been a lifetime affliction that demands a root cause—a common enemy who has mistreated both women and children to preserve what? A secret balloon experiment? Wooden crash dummies? Place yourself in the shoes of those who actually lived it. Just what type of parents would will their own sons and daughters both the physical and emotional anguish as reward for simply having the name Brazel, Marcel, Proctor, or a dozen other examples? Imagine that these are your children that you are about to meet. At the very least, it should leave you contemplating: Suppose they *are* right?

CHAPTER 1

"This Is Where Mack Found Something Else"

*I*f we are to continue to believe the present scenario maintained by the U.S. Air Force, 48-year-old ranch foreman Mack Brazel, accompanied by his 8-year-old son, Vernon, discovered wreckage of a downed Mogul balloon train on Saturday, June 14, 1947. Far from impressed with the remnants of something quite prosaic in nature, he rode on and continued his routine chores. He would describe the debris as "large area of bright wreckage made up of rubber strips, tinfoil, a rather tough paper and sticks."[1] Brazel, his wife, Margaret, Vernon, and his daughter, Bessie, would return to collect the material three weeks later on Friday, the Fourth of July. This sole account of events is based on a July 9, 1947, *Roswell Daily Record* front-page newspaper story and subsequent Project Mogul report from 1994. So we continue to be misled….

From all eyewitness accounts, this is precisely what chronologically happened. Based on newly discovered historical weather records from Stallion Army Air Field, New Mexico, a severe thunderstorm roared through the Corona, New Mexico, region late on the evening of Wednesday, July 2, 1947. Residents through the area reported the sound of an explosion between the thunder claps. The very next morning, Mack Brazel, inspecting the J.B. Foster ranch, came upon an expansive debris field about 8 miles south of the ranch house. Stepping down from his horse, he immediately observed that the scattering material was highly unusual and covered such a vast area that he also became concerned as to who was responsible to dispose of it. Over the next three days, Brazel alerted everyone he could to the unusual event and sought their advice as what to do about it. A few of his neighbors informed him about the recent flying saucer sightings and, according to everyone who handled samples from the debris field, this seemed like an outside possibility. And as the weathered rancher hopped into the old, run-down pickup truck to inform the authorities in Roswell, we're sure good-old Mack had little notion of how his entire life was about to change—as well as the lives of all those around him, especially a young boy they called "Dee," for it wasn't Vernon, Mack's son, who rode up with him onto that pasture with all of that strange wreckage, as was originally falsely reported by the press. In reality, it was 7-year-old Timothy "Dee" Proctor, the third son of his nearest neighbors, Floyd and Loretta Proctor.[2]

Young Dee was no stranger to tending sheep and cattle. As many old-timers described early in our investigation, ranchers' sons are put in a saddle as soon as they are able to walk. Dee was no exception, and numerous neighbors confirmed that he spent summers and weekends riding the range with Brazel. At times, much to the consternation of the adults, his over-enthusiasm was often fearless, as he would ride out ahead on his own with nary a care of a rattlesnake or sinkhole down the trail. During the summer of 1947, there were no ranch hands hired to assist Brazel, but the little Proctor boy eagerly worked for a mere 25 cents per day.[3]

Life in the Corona area was rough and dusty, and friends were separated by 10 miles and more. Ranch work was principally done on horseback, and the desert sun was unrelenting as it pounded a daily drumbeat on horse and rider. Most ranches had no electricity, no telephone service, and no running water. Still, the young "cowboys" were anxious for summer break from school so they could live out the adventures of the Old West they read about. But the tale of southwestern cow "boys" finding a flying saucer, that was a book yet to be written.

Brazel gathered a few pieces of the unknown metal and stuffed them in his saddlebag. He had promised the Proctors to have Dee home for the weekend holiday festivities, so the two of them headed to the neighboring ranch. Mack stepped down from his horse and handed his neighbors a small piece of the material. It was about 4 inches long, round, and as light as balsa wood. Loretta Proctor told us she "didn't know what the stuff was." It resembled plastic, "but it wasn't plastic." She described how her husband tried to whittle on it with his pocketknife and couldn't make a mark on it. Brazel himself held a match up to it to show that it wouldn't even turn black. As much as Brazel encouraged them to check out the site themselves, they declined. In 1989, Loretta told us, "We should have gone, but gas and tires were expensive then. We had our chores and it would have been 20 miles round trip."[4] But their son had other plans.

All of that funny-looking metal was just out in the middle of nowhere for the taking. Brazel wanted someone to clear it up; he wouldn't miss a piece or two. And who would know if some obliging friends came along—something to do? After all, the annual rodeo down in Capitan wasn't until the next day.

Over the course of the next few days, while Brazel was hitting his head against the wall searching for answers, neighboring ranchers one-by-one made their way to the newest local attraction. Souvenirs were taken and hidden with the realization this was something special—out of the ordinary. Nevertheless, daily chores needed to be completed, even over a holiday weekend. Dee stopped by to help, but this time he had company. Their surnames were Wright, Edington, and Pierce; all were about the same age as Dee. Mack's son, Vernon, was also there when he made the ultimate discovery: a small craft of unknown origin, which had deposited a great amount of wreckage over that open arroyo, had a crew![5] Brazel would call them "poor unfortunate creatures."[6] This was too much for any of them to comprehend. For the Proctor boy and his posse of young riders, the rope was about to tighten and pull them back down to earth.

Whatever Dee and the others saw back in July 1947, according to his mother, Loretta, "He was white as a ghost. He would never talk about it again." And then she added something that both the Air Force and earlier investigators got wrong. It wasn't Brazel's son, Vernon, who was with him when he first discovered the debris field. And Mack wasn't alone. "My son Dee was with old Mack when he found that thing. He was 7 back then," confessed Loretta. When first we had the opportunity to meet and ask Dee about the incident, he sounded quite agitated and remarked, "I wasn't even born back then!" which was quite a surprise to his mother.[7] It immediately became evident that then-40-year-old Dee Proctor would be joining the ranks of our other reluctant witnesses. And he was willing to go so far as to make his own mother out to be a liar.[8]

But Loretta was telling us the truth, and we can assure readers that we immediately realized that we had a potential witness who could answer all of the relevant questions about the entire affair—most importantly, were there indeed bodies?—an admission that would render any weather balloon explanation by the Air Force as totally irrelevant. Yet, the very same unknown powers who left a trail of fear and intimidation in the likes of Dee Proctor, later served as the same obstacle to us. Such was the lifetime of obfuscation imposed on Dee that he refused to speak with any members of his own family as well—including his mother and father. Whenever we sought help from his own siblings, they, too, lamented the same reaction they observed each and every time the subject came up: Dee would immediately change the subject or flee their very presence. We would meet with his brother Norris, not to mention his sisters Loretta and Alma. Traveling all the way to Great Falls, Montana, we even spoke with his uncle Robert Porter. None of them could share any information about Dee. He would have no part of any line of questioning from any of them about what happened back in 1947.[9]

Dee had been married and divorced by the time we first were introduced to him at the original Proctor homestead in 1989. This was the same ranch house to which Mack Brazel returned the then-7-year-old boy back in 1947. As often as we would call, we were always told he wasn't there. On one occasion, we stopped by at Loretta Proctor's invitation in an attempt to get her son to talk. No sooner than we were invited into the front room, we heard the rear door slam. Within moments we observed Dee race his pickup down the driveway away from the house. "I guess he doesn't want to talk to you," his mother dejectedly said. One more time we stopped by, totally unannounced. Loretta was a bit uneasy and wasn't sure if her son was home or not. We couldn't help but notice Dee's truck parked out front. Just as the conversation couldn't have gotten any more awkward, who should walk into the room, still in a bathrobe for a late-morning breakfast, but our evasive fugitive, one Timothy Dee Proctor? Unfortunately for us, the moment he made eye contact with us, he reacted like a wanted criminal, quickly spun and hurriedly fled the room without muttering a word. "Now I know he doesn't want to talk to you," his mother smugly remarked.[10] Failing again, we had to try other measures. He was too important to solving the case.

For months, we met with anyone around the Corona region we could find who knew anything about the crash. They all knew Dee. Although we learned more and more about the general atmosphere of what transpired in the summer of 1947, one overriding theme crept back to torment our efforts time and time again: Dee refused to talk about his involvement to anyone. We could find no exceptions. Oh yes, he was there with Mack Brazel. Oh yes, "he saw everything" as longtime neighbor Mary Ann Strickland commented, and "He won't ever talk to you," said everybody else.[11] It was as though they all had given up on that notion themselves. What about his closest friends? It was becoming our experience that, in an attempt to protect their families, witnesses in sensitive situations often confide to outside individuals.

We enlisted Lincoln County Deputy Sheriff Lerry D. Bond and Magistrate Judge Gary McDaniel of Farmington, New Mexico. As close as they were to Dee, they remained totally in the dark. But each one tried repeatedly to pry the slightest tidbit from their friend. And just as we had, they finally concluded that he possessed a secret so dark, and so deep, that his fears of retaliation exceeded any fame or fortune.[12] But we were patient and hoped at best for a slow trickle of the truth—a truth that only Dee kept locked away.

Floyd and Loretta Proctor in the 1940s.

After his father, Floyd, had passed away in 1967, the rest of the family kept an eye on Dee. Through the years the demons took their toll as he took to the bottle more and more, and alcohol became his daily crutch. Dee ate to excess until his weight became a total hindrance to performing any ranch duties; he wouldn't enjoy riding a horse again for most of his adult life. His marriage was tumultuous and left him devoid of self-esteem. He would move in back home with Loretta and became more and more of a recluse. The carefree, adventurous little boy, who was forced to face a reality one only reads about in works of fiction, had long ago died. And what had robbed him back in 1947 of his innocent spirit was not anything from outer space. It had a very earthly origin.[13]

Just imagine a scenario where there is a major breech of security: The military is forced to take immediate action against civilians, which in itself is a constitutional felony. Now, what if children are also involved? What type of a cold-hearted individual does one have to be to threaten innocent children with the possibility of never seeing their families again? Certainly, if the concern was just over exotic pieces of metal from a crashed aircraft, a firm, simple reminder that the "stuff's top secret, and it's your patriotic duty to keep your mouth shut," would suffice. What else did Dee Proctor, Mack Brazel, and the others see that required the most extreme measures to ensure their cooperation? What could a 7-year-old see that would force the government that is sworn to protect him to threaten him in the most boorish way for seeing something the government decided we shouldn't have seen then and still have yet to see today? What type of fear does one instill in a child, a child no different than one's own, and then walk away—no counseling, no gentle persuasion, no lifting of a lifetime of intimidation and fear? Remaining is a lasting image destroyed by grownups, who today commit the ultimate crime against the children of Roswell by still insisting that it was all over a weather balloon.

It would take a life-threatening situation involving Dee's mother, Loretta, to instigate a brief revelation. In 1994, a blood clot was discovered in Loretta's carotid artery inside her neck. As her doctor monitored her condition, the entire family was informed of the severity of the situation. Within a few days, Dee returned home. No sooner than he walked in the door, Dee announced to Loretta, "Mom, I need to take you someplace. I need to show you something." Maybe Dee felt it might be his last and only chance, but after coaxing Loretta a little longer, she finally agreed to get into his truck and see what he was so anxious for her to see.

All of the dirt roads they traveled brought back a lifetime of memories and, given her condition, the thought that it might be the last time momentarily crossed Loretta's mind. It appeared they were headed to the old Foster ranch, and as her son turned onto the old Hines Draw Road, just 3 miles from "ground zero" of the 1947 incident, Loretta seriously wondered if Dee would finally tell her—show her—the truth. But then a strange thing happened: Dee didn't make the turn onto the two-track horse trail to where the old windmill stood watch over that historic site. They kept going. They missed the turn as Loretta silently mused to herself, "Where is my boy taking me?"[14]

Hines Draw Road is a graded, gravel county road serving all the surrounding ranches in the area. It twists and turns before coming to a fork. To the left leads to the old Foster ranch house. To the right is what is still called the "twin mills," where two windmills pump what little water there is hundreds of feet below the desert surface. Dee headed toward the sheep pen, stepped from the truck, unwrapped the chain securing the gate, and gasped for breath as he climbed back behind the steering wheel. After proceeding on seldom-used trails almost too faint to see, and 10 minutes more bouncing up and down on the stony trail, they came to another gate. From there they drove into the next pasture and past the first of two bluffs, before swinging around and up and over before coming to a stop above the second bluff. By that time Loretta was more confused than ever, yet she still hoped that Dee was about to make up for all those years of silence. Dee struggled as he helped Loretta down from the seat and stepped ahead of the vehicle. As they glanced out over the edge of the large rocky bluff, the wind picked up as they stood in the early spring sun. Dee then took her by the hand, looked her in the eyes, and said, "Mom, this is where Mack found *something else.*" Not another word was said. Loretta had a dozen other questions. Nonetheless she cherished the all-too-cryptic confession. She knew exactly what her son meant. This was where *he* also found something else. And some of the weight he carried all those years had been lifted. It wasn't any weather balloon, she knew that to be true, and Dee just assured her of that fact. Peering off to the west along the horizon, they both could see the single windmill on the eastern edge of the debris field, a couple of miles away.

The "Dee Proctor Site" bluff, where several dead aliens were found who had been blown out of their crippled ship when it exploded. Photo from 2012.

Some months later, after surgery had cleared up Loretta's condition and she was recovering, she directed us to the same location she and Dee had visited. Little did she know that we had been to the precise spot many times, beginning five years earlier. Juanita Sultemeier had described Army trucks with large spotlights driving down the "twin mills" trail at the time of the incident. Other ranchers had described going through the two gates and how, within that separate pasture, Mack Brazel, in the company of a group of young boys, had discovered some remains from the crash. Two local researchers in Roswell had also encouraged us to explore the talk about a secondary site a couple of miles from the wreckage field. Still, the one source that brought it all together and had taken us to precisely Dee's location was the then–ranch supervisor, Jeff Wells.[15] Wells was of tremendous assistance to us during the first five years of our independent Roswell investigation. Not only did he know every rancher within the county, he also knew what roles they played among the other cast of characters. And from all that he could gather about 1947 in private discussions with those folks, he was able to take us to that same location—the secondary body site that, since that time, we have always respectfully referred to as the "Dee Proctor Site."

Later that fall (1994), we were filming with the British Broadcasting Corporation (BBC) under the direction of award-winning producer, John Purdy. As part of that day's schedule, we had Loretta escort us, while riding in the lead vehicle, back out to that bluff where Dee had taken her. That was the final confirmation we needed, short of Dee himself. It was official: There was indeed a second site connected to the same incident just 2 1/2 miles east–southeast from the original site discovered by Mack Brazel in the company of Dee and the others.[16] But Loretta, now that she was recovered, felt that her son would once again slam the door shut, and pretend as before that he was never involved. Unfortunately, she was absolutely correct. It appeared as though we had gotten about all we would ever get from Dee, but all was not lost, if not for a chance phone call.

Author Tom Carey atop the "Dee Proctor Site" pointing to where the alien crew members had likely met their demise, 2012.

Time passed, and after a couple of years, Kevin Randle had a follow-up question for Loretta. Serendipitously, Dee answered the phone and actually engaged the Roswell researcher, who was not about to miss this chance opportunity. According to Randle, the reclusive Dee finally admitted to the following:

∠ He was with Mack Brazel on the early morning of Thursday, July 3, 1947.

∠ He and Mack Brazel came upon a large field of metallic-like debris.

∠ He and a number of unnamed friends later went out to the site.

∠ Military officials privately talked with him about the crash.

∠ The crash debris was not man-made. It was not from this earth.[17]

That was all that Dee would admit, and that was as far as the conversation went. Nevertheless, everything that he acknowledged was what we had already suspected. As much as we would have liked to believe that there was still time to get a full confession, fate had other plans for Dee, as his health continued to decline. On his way to visit a ranch friend in Ruidoso, New Mexico, Dee suffered a massive heart attack on January 22, 2006. He was just 66 years old.

While Dee's last companion, two sons, three brothers, and four sisters continue the same reluctance to talk about any matters related to 1947, some have taken it a step further. They now repeat the skeptic's party line that the wreckage was nothing more than "junk," and that Dee, as a mere 7-year-old at the time of the incident, was too young to be impressed by any of it. They maintain that Dee openly talked about the affair and never claimed it was of an extraordinary nature. Not true, as we were the ones, time and time again, that he made every effort to flee from. Not true, if Loretta Proctor, who was closer to her son Dee than any of these, pointed us in his direction in the first place. Not true, if other neighbors and friends of his also confirmed the negative effect the incident had on his life. Not true, based on Dee's own final admissions, which specifically detail and confirm the significance of the entire affair.

Roswell Witness Conference, Washington, DC, May 1990. Left to right: Dr. Bruce Maccabee, Stanton Friedman, Vern Maltais, Hans Adam II, and Don Schmitt.

In 1990 Prince Hans Adam II of Liechtenstein presented Loretta Proctor with a priceless collection of commemorative stamps from his nation, a personal testimony that he applauded her family's involvement in what he told us was "one of the most significant events of all time."[18] Thirty years before, Professor Richard Glaze, head of the agriculture department at the New Mexico State University at Las Cruces, recipient of the Distinguished Service Award, after a visit with the Proctor family, left a brief note, which read: "If you find anything unusual, let me know."[19] Floyd, Loretta, and Dee are all gone now, and the hope of finding anything "unusual" is forever gone too.

True, we did fail to get a full confession from a potential witness who could have painted us a Roswell masterpiece. Short of Mack Brazel himself, Dee Proctor was the only civilian witness who experienced both the wreckage and "something else." But children will often allow the monsters under the bed to accompany them throughout their lives. Unfortunately, for Dee and us, his boogeymen wore suits and carried government credentials.

CHAPTER 2

"I Never Saw My Father So Scared"

*T*oday, we refer to threats made by members of the military against civilians as civil rights violations or war crimes if committed in time of war, and their perpetrators would be brought to a swift justice and punished severely. Especially when such acts involve excesses by the military establishment upon the helpless, whether military or civilian—the resulting outrage by the media can reach firestorm proportions. Military reprisals against civilians, even in times of war and against enemy civilians (e.g., the so-called 1968 "Mỹ Lai Massacre" of local civilians by U.S. troops in Vietnam), is repugnant to our value system, something that will not be tolerated by the United States citizenry.

Occurring as it did sometime during the first week of July 1947, the Roswell Incident happened at the time of the first wave of flying saucer sightings around the country that summer. The latest "sighting of the day" commanded front-page attention in most newspapers, as was the case with events in Roswell. As an anxious and excited nation—and world—awaited more news of the discovery, things were about to change. Moving quickly to kill the story, the U.S. government used a combination of appeals to patriotism, claims of "national security," bribery, threats of long prison sentences, and outright thuggery in the form of death threats to contain the story. An innocuous, downed weather balloon was offered up to the press by the Air Force as the cause of the furor. It was all just a case of mistaken identity by the men of the 509th Bomb Group in Roswell, men who apparently could not tell the difference between an extraterrestrial spaceship and a mundane weather balloon. It should have sent a chill down everyone's spine, because it was the men of the 509th Bomb Group who ended World War II by dropping the atomic bombs on Hiroshima and Nagasaki, and in 1947 was the only nuclear strike force in the world with their fingers still gripping the atomic trigger. But most were not aware of that connection. As a result, the Roswell Incident became just a two-day story in the media and was quickly forgotten.

Those in the military who were involved in the retrieval of the wreckage, the bodies, and what was left infact of the crashed UFO itself were the easiest to deal with. Roswell Army Air Field was a Strategic Air Command (SAC) base, so everyone who worked there, military and civilian alike, was already familiar with the base policy of not talking about things that went on at the base, even to family members—*ever*. To drive home this point, the enlisted men involved in the cleanup at the various sites were detained in groups and "debriefed" (sworn to secrecy under the guise of national security). Long prison terms were promised in case anyone was thinking of talking, and we have also heard that bribes of $10,000 or more were used to assure the silence of those who saw the bodies (e.g., Staff Sergeant Melvin E. Brown). The officers involved, especially career officers, were less of a problem. In order to advance a career in the military, one does not defy orders or breach security. One key officer, Major Edwin Easley, who was heavily involved in the recovery operations, even promised President Truman (via Truman's aide) that he would keep the secret forever.[1] He did until he was on his deathbed many years later. Controlling civilians, however, was a different matter.

Except in time of war or under conditions when Martial Law has been declared under the Constitution, the U.S. military has no direct authority over the civilian population. The military could keep its own house (the men of 509th Bomb Group stationed in Roswell and up the chain of command) quiet, but how to keep the civilians from exercising their God-given, Bill of Rights–guaranteed freedom of speech? And there were a lot of civilians involved in the Roswell Incident all along the way: from the initial discovery of pieces of wreckage and strange little bodies by civilians near Corona, to the discovery of the intact part of the craft just to the north of Roswell, to the recovery operations at the Roswell base itself, and finally to the shipment of the wreckage and bodies to Wright Field in Dayton, Ohio.

Aside from the ranchers living between Roswell and the little town of Corona whose homes were indiscriminately ransacked in the military's mad search for "souvenirs" from the crash[2], and the rancher, Mack Brazel, who started it all and who was dealt with directly by the military, other civilians involved in the 1947 Roswell events were dealt with through civilian authority figures. The highest-ranking of these was Dennis Chavez, the junior U.S. senator from New Mexico. He was "enlisted" by the Army Air Forces to intimidate Roswell radio station KGFL, whose ownership had secured an exclusive, recorded interview of Mack Brazel, during which Brazel told of finding strange wreckage and the bodies of "little people." Walt Whitmore, Sr., the station's majority owner, was threatened by Senator Chavez with the loss of the station's broadcasting license if it went ahead with its plans to air the Brazel interview (KGFL had planned to "scoop" the other Roswell media outlets with the interview). KGFL's minority owner, Jud Roberts, was similarly threatened, and, for good measure, the head of the Federal Communications Commission in Washington, DC, T.J. Slowie, also threatened Whitmore and Roberts with the same message. It worked better than was hoped for, as Whitmore caved completely by not only turning over the taped Brazel interview, but also by becoming a willing accomplice in the military's campaign to silence civilians. One of KGFL's announcers, Frank Joyce, had also been called by "a military person in Washington" and was "read the riot act" to shut up about the crash. Joyce had been the first media person to interview Brazel and knew Brazel's original story, including the part about his finding little bodies. Incensed about being told what to do by someone in the military, Joyce let him know what he could do. The angry voice in Washington shot back, "I'll show what I can do!" and hung up. A day or two later, Joyce's boss, Walt Whitmore, Sr., told Joyce to get into his car and go for a ride with him. Joyce did so, and then noticed a strange-looking man in a strange-looking uniform sitting in the back seat. The man did not speak. Whitmore drove north out of Roswell for more than an hour to a remote shack off the Corona Road. He was told by Whitmore to get out of the car and go into the shack. This Joyce did, still not knowing what was going on. Joyce stood alone in the shack for a few minutes, wondering what was taking place, when in walked none other than Mack Brazel himself. "You're not going to say anything about what I told you the other day, are you?" Brazel pleaded more than asked Joyce. "Not if you don't want me to," responded Joyce. "Good. You know our lives will never be the same." With that, Brazel turned around and walked out, and Joyce never laid eyes on him again. Joyce then returned to Whitmore's car for the ride back to Roswell, and noticed that the stranger in the back seat was gone. Apparently the military was *still* not sufficiently convinced by Joyce's pledge not to say anything, as he was shortly thereafter gathered up and physically removed to a military hospital in Texas for the next year or so under circumstances that are still not clear to him. A Roswell native, Joyce did not return to Roswell upon his release, returning only many years later, upon his death, where he remains today.[3]

Chaves County Sheriff George Wilcox was the main local authority figure utilized by the Army Air Forces on the ground in Roswell to help contain the story. A picture of him on the telephone, looking like a deer caught in the headlights, was prominently featured on the front page of the July 9, 1947, edition of the *Roswell Daily Record*. But Wilcox was doing more than just answering telephone calls. He refused to give any details to inquiries regarding what was going on, because he was just "helping out the fellows over at the base."[4] He also completely rolled over in the face of the military full court press by allowing himself to be used as the enforcer to intimidate local Roswellians into keeping their mouths shut about what they witnessed. It was his task to deliver the threat of the ultimate sanction to those who saw or knew about the bodies recovered from the crash.

Glenn Dennis, a Roswell mortician, allegedly knew about the bodies from a nurse friend who was involved in the autopsy of one of them at the base. Dennis had been threatened at the base hospital by an officer and, like Frank Joyce, Dennis became incensed at his treatment by the officer and told him where he might go. The next day, Dennis's father received a visit from Sheriff Wilcox and a deputy to tell him that his son "was in trouble at the base."[5] No doubt the veiled death threat of the previous day was part of the message delivered by Wilcox.

In 1947, future U.S. Senator Joseph Montoya was the lieutenant governor of New Mexico and was on the Roswell airbase for another function when the wreckage and little bodies from the UFO crash started arriving at the Big Hangar (Hangar P-3). As the state's highest-ranking official on-site, he was called to the hangar to see what was going on. The sight of the alien wreckage and especially the little bodies with big heads was too much for him. So, he called some of the *Montoyistas* (young political supporters of Montoya) whom he knew in Roswell (Pete and Ruben Anaya) to come to the base and, "Get me the hell out of here!" They drove him to Pete Anaya's house, where Montoya proceeded to get drunk, but not before telling the Anayas about the "spaceship" and the "little bodies with big heads."

Because Pete Anaya worked on the base in a civilian capacity, he was recognized when he came to pick up Montoya. So the Air Force got Sheriff Wilcox, who spoke Spanish fluently, to deliver the death threat to the Anayas, figuring that Montoya had told the Anayas about what he had seen.[6]

According to Pete Anaya and his wife Mary, who were interviewed again in September 2002 about this incident, Wilcox delivered the ultimate sanction to them if they talked about what they knew: "If you say anything, you will be killed. And your entire family will be killed as well."[7] It is not known to how many others Sheriff Wilcox delivered this message on behalf of the Army, but what is known is that he never ran for sheriff again. According to family and friends, the Roswell events "destroyed him." Now, we know why. When asked about all this just a few years ago, a former deputy of Wilcox's responded, "I don't want to get shot."[8] After the story had been contained, and things had died down a bit, the Army paid a visit to Sheriff Wilcox and his wife, Inez. To praise or reward him for a nasty job well done, you may ask? Think again. The message delivered to the startled couple was that unless they kept quiet about everything, not only would they be killed, but their children would also be killed.[9] Sheriff Wilcox died in 1961. Asked by her granddaughter years later whether she believed the threats or not, Inez Wilcox looked at her with a straight face and clear eyes, and said, "What do you think?"

In July 2008, the International UFO Museum in Roswell had a visit from a native Roswellian woman now living on the East Coast. And she had an interesting story to tell, one that she had kept hidden within herself for years. Like so many others who have visited the museum over the years, being there somehow provided the cathartic boost to allow her to talk about suppressed and repressed unpleasant memories.

Sue Farnsworth had never seen her father with such a frightened look on his face before in her young life during the summer of 1947. After all, Arthur Farnsworth was a successful and prominent businessman who owned and managed Roswell's original Ford dealership, Roswell Auto Co., located at the intersection of West 2nd St. and Richardson Ave., in downtown Roswell. He was a pillar of the community. Besides their home at 612 N. Richardson Ave., the Farnsworths also owned a working ranch northwest of Roswell that the family frequented as a "getaway." Arthur, especially, was known to visit the ranch several times a week. Seven year-old Sue Farnsworth had two older sisters, both of whom had polio, and it was Sue who became "best buddies" with her father, by helping out with the ranch chores and sharing important father/daughter matters with each other when the need arose. "We were used to finding 'funny things' from White Sands on our ranch all the time, but this was clearly something different judging by the military reaction."[10] Unable to contain her concern for her father any longer, Sue finally asked him what was wrong one day when they were out at the ranch. Without saying a word, he motioned to her to follow him. He then mounted a horse, as did she, and they rode out to a remote and secluded part of the ranch, whereupon they dismounted. According to Sue, "Whenever we wanted to discuss something without anyone else hearing, we would go to this spot."

Like everyone else, Sue had heard the stories and rumors about the UFO crash that were rife at the time, but she was not prepared for what her father was about to confide to her. Like so many times before, Sue and her father sat down on their favorite rock and stared out over the peaceful, scrub-desert landscape. "Your father was threatened by the military a few days ago," Arthur Farnsworth told his daughter. Looking around carefully even though they were out in the middle of nowhere, Arthur Farnsworth continued in a low voice, "What I tell you now you must never tell anyone. A *flying saucer* crashed on another ranch near here, and the military told us that if we ever said anything to anyone about it, they would kill all of us. I went out there with some other ranchers soon after word of the crash got around, and we saw some things we weren't supposed to see." Arthur Farnsworth did not go into any detail with his young daughter. "Remember: not a word—to anyone!" That was all he would ever reveal to her. The two then saddled up and rode back to the ranch house, never to speak of the matter again.

We can speculate now what probably happened to Arthur Farnsworth to cause him to fear for his life and the lives of his family. He and the other ranchers whom he was with must have gotten a fairly good look at not only the physical crash wreckage, but also the alien bodies. Terminal threats were reserved for civilians who had witnessed the latter. Most likely, Farnsworth had visited one of the body sites (either the "Dee Proctor Site" on the Foster Ranch in Lincoln County or the "Impact Site" in Chaves County, much closer to Roswell) shortly after the crash on one of the days that he was out as his ranch. News of the crash traveled like a flash among the ranchers—even in those days—and ranchers with their excited children *always* got to airplane crash sites before the authorities. It was no different with the crash of a UFO.

Upon hearing news of the crash, Arthur Farnsworth, with his neighboring ranchers, headed for the crash site to see for themselves. This would have been sometime between July 3rd (the day following the crash the previous night) and July 7th (the day that the military started securing the crash sites with armed MPs). George Cisneros, now 94 years old, still lives on the same ranch he lived on in 1947 near the town of Arabela, New Mexico, about 20 miles from the Foster Ranch where Mack Brazel was the foreman. According to Cisneros, who did not go to any of the UFO crash sites himself, a number of his neighbors *did*. When we asked him if his neighbors reported seeing anything, his response was, "Hell, yes!

When they came back, everyone was excited and buzzing about a crashed spaceship and 'little space people.'"[11] If Arthur Farnsworth was among them or with a different group of ranchers who visited one of the two crash sites with bodies, he no doubt saw the same things. Perhaps the military arrived at the crash site soon thereafter and issued a stern warning to everyone, including Farnsworth. Or, perhaps a few days or weeks after that, he was paid a visit by another military officer, such as the "brutal" Hunter Penn whose job it was to conduct a sweep of the ranches near the crash sites to enforce the silence of those ranchers who knew too much about the crash—and especially about the bodies.[12] As we have discussed, the threat of "terminal action" was authorized to secure compliance. In the words of Sue Farnsworth, 62 years after the fact, "I never in my life saw my father so scared, before or since."[13]

Getting rough with people was just the style of Army Air Forces officer Hunter Penn. In 2008, our associate Anthony Bragalia located and interviewed the foster daughter of retired Air Force Colonel Hunter G. Penn (now deceased). During World War II, Penn was a bombardier on a bomber in the 303rd Bomb Group known as "Hell's Angels." Curiously, according to unit records, Penn was pulled from flight status after just two missions for unknown reasons. After the war, she said that he was "associated" with Wright Field, and that when she was a teenager her foster father told her that he had undertaken a deadly serious assignment back in the summer of 1947. He explained to her that when he was at Wright Field, he was ordered to "visit ranches around Roswell, New Mexico," close to where a UFO had crashed that summer.[14] She told Bragalia that her foster father was "tasked" (to put it euphemistically) to "help manage civilian-military affairs after the crash," to ensure that an "information blackout" regarding the event was put—and kept—in force. More bluntly, he was to question those who might know something about the crash, especially the little bodies, and "make sure they did not talk."

Hunter Penn was ordered to concentrate on ranchers, farmers, and "simple types" residing in the outlying areas between Roswell and Corona who may have seen something, using intimidation and threats (with a weapon) to instill fear and compliance. The matter was so important, Penn told his foster daughter, that he was authorized to use physical force, including weaponry, on non-compliant people to enforce their silence. He confirmed to her that the crash near Roswell was extraterrestrial, and that they were concerned at the time about the unknown dangers or problems that might be in the offing[15], thus independently echoing the deathbed declaration of the former Roswell Army Air Field (RAAF) base adjutant, Major Patrick H. Saunders, "We didn't know where they were from, or what their intentions were."[16]

Because of Michelle Penn's willingness to talk to Anthony Bragalia, we now know of the "dirty work" that her foster father, a former Army Air Forces officer from the notorious "Hell's Angels" Bomb Squadron in the ETO (European Theater of Operations) during World War II, inflicted upon innocent civilians in the wake of the Roswell UFO crash.

While she was growing up, Hunter Penn's foster daughter, Michelle, said she was fearful of her alcoholic foster father ("He was a brutal person."), and she didn't need to be told never to say anything about what he had recounted to her about his involvement at Roswell in 1947. To this day, she is not sure *why* he told her, but it may have been his way of "parenting" by using a fear factor to instill a desired result in the behavioral control over a child. She said that she was made to address him as "Sir" as a child. According to Michelle, her foster-father was also "brutal" with her alcoholic foster-mother, Elinore. The bottom line here is that Michelle Penn believes that her foster-father was entrusted with the role of being a "bad cop" by the Air Force when the situation called for it, because he was known as being brutally tough with people—just what was needed at Roswell.

In more dramatic terms, "He tried to 'heart-attack' people!" Michelle said that her father would also sometimes brandish a military pick axe (similar to an ice pick). She thinks that he was obsessed by picks and believes that he may have used one at Roswell.[17]

In the weeks and months immediately following the Roswell UFO crash, after the initial fervor had died down, the question of how to maintain and enforce the silence of those who knew the truth became a paramount issue. Apparently, it was felt that appeals of "national security" and "patriotism" would not be enough to achieve the desired result of complete silence, especially on the part of the outlying ranchers. In the military mindset of the time, the answer was to "Put the fear of God in them!"[18] Enter Hunter G. Penn and the look on the face of Sue Farnsworth's father.

CHAPTER 3

"It Was Horrifying for My Family"

Sunday was Chaves County's 53-year-old sheriff George M. Wilcox's usual day off, time to relax, and time to spend with family: his wife, Inez; their daughter, Phyllis (McGuire); and Phyllis's young son, George[1]—if that was possible for a county sheriff to do, especially one who lived on the top floor of the county courthouse that also housed the county jail. At that time, part of the sheriff's job description was that his wife had to prepare the meals for the prisoners "residing" in the jail. He hoped Sunday, July 6, 1947, would be a quiet one. Although not reported in the Roswell's two daily newspapers, the *Daily Record* and the *Morning Dispatch,* something strange was going on in the world that would ruin his day and ultimately change his life forever.

For the previous two weeks there had been reports in the national newswires and on radio broadcasts of strange things, dubbed "flying saucers" by the press, that people were seeing cavorting about in the skies above.[2] The state of New Mexico and the city of Roswell especially seemed to be bearing the brunt of this aerial "invasion." In future years, UFO historians would refer to these periods of increased UFO activity as "flaps" (e.g., the 1947, 1952, and 1957 "flaps"). Gallup Polls taken at the time revealed that most people believed these things to be secret military developments of the United States, the Soviet Union, or even Germany.[3] Way down the list of possibilities was that they might be "interplanetary" (the

1940s equivalent of today's term *extraterrestrial*) in origin. Unknown to Sheriff Wilcox or anyone else at the time, it was the dawn of the Modern Age of UFOs.

Deputy sheriff B.A. "Bernie" Clarke had the duty that hot July 4th holiday weekend. It was central New Mexico's "monsoon season," which featured intense thunder and lightning storms with or without accompanying rain, as sometimes the air was so hot that what rain there was evaporated before reaching the ground. Clarke had internalized his instructions from Sheriff Wilcox that he (Wilcox) should only be disturbed in the case of emergency or something out of the ordinary that might require his personal attention.

Wilcox's 35-year-old chief deputy, Leslie O. "Tommy" Thompson, a bear of a man, was also enjoying the privileges of rank by having the weekend off. Years later, during an interview we had with him in the living room of his Roswell home, Thompson would tell us that Wilcox had been a "laid back" administrator, and that it was he (Thompson) who actually ran the day-to-day operations of the sheriff's office. Yet, having said that, Thompson incredibly then claimed to know *nothing* at all about the Roswell UFO events of early July 1947—truly unbelievable, to say the least. Later, we heard back from our go-between person who had arranged our meeting with Thompson. He told us that after we left, he had stayed a little while longer with Thompson as a courtesy to our "quarry." He then revealed to us that, after we left, Thompson had asked him half-jokingly, "Well, how'd I do?" To which our meeting-arranger advised Thompson, "Well, Tommy, you gave the boys [Carey and Schmitt] an opening. First you told them that you were the one who really ran the place [the sheriff's office]. Then you told them that you don't know and never heard *anything* about it [the 1947 incident], which is hard for anyone to believe." To which Thompson sheepishly responded, "*Ooops!*"[4]

In the end, we never could get Tommy Thompson to "fess up." After 1947, he would go on to become chief of police for the City of Roswell, later taking Wilcox's old job as sheriff of Chaves County, and finally serving as magistrate of Chaves County. Thompson retired from public service in 1982.

After Thompson's interviews with us, he moved to Texas to spend his final years near his children. He passed away in December 2007 at the age of 95, taking everything he knew about the Roswell UFO incident of 1947—which had to be plenty—with him to his grave. It recalls a story about Thompson told to us by long-time friends of his, Jack Rodden and Glenn Dennis, when we first asked them about Thompson.[5] They had approached Thompson themselves early on, inquiring of him what he might know about the 1947 events. *"They'd blow my head off if I told you!"* Thompson bellowed back at them. And that was that. End of conversation. The question of just who "they" were was never answered, nor even asked. Was he just being stubborn, "blowing smoke," or keeping a promise? Rumor had it that Thompson had been paid off by the government to remain silent. We had heard that before regarding other "key" witnesses, such as the rancher Mack Brazel.

On the front page of the July 9, 1947 edition of the *Roswell Daily Record*, above the fold, was a picture of Sheriff George Wilcox with a "deer-in-the-headlights" look on his face as he was talking on the telephone. The caption under the photo stated that Wilcox had handled telephone calls from all over the world in response to the previous day's press release that the Roswell Army Air Field (RAAF) had "captured a flying saucer." One or two other newspaper accounts quoted sheriff Wilcox as stating that he was "...just helping out the boys over at the base [by fielding—and deflecting—the spate of calls by telling the callers that he knew nothing]."[6] As followers of the Roswell case already know, the Air Force reversed itself only scant hours after the initial press release with the infamous "Ramey press conference" of July 8, 1947, in Fort Worth, Texas[7], where it was claimed that what had crashed near Roswell was not a flying saucer. It was just a common, everyday weather balloon that had bamboozled the boys of the 509th Bomb Group over in Roswell—boys with their fingers on the atomic trigger[8]—boys who could not tell the difference between neoprene rubber, balsa-wood sticks, and baling twine from an interplanetary spaceship capable of navigating the universe! Without flinching, the national news media unquestioningly accepted this "explanation" and immediately dropped the Roswell story, rendering it as just a one or two-day blip, depending upon whether you lived east or west of the Mississippi River, in an otherwise-crazy summer season. George Wilcox passed away in 1961 at the age of 67, and it would be years before the true nature of *le affaire Roswell* and his role in it would be revealed.

It did not become known in the first book dedicated to the Roswell Incident, *The Roswell Incident,* published in 1980, as Sheriff Wilcox was only briefly mentioned in passing regarding his initial meeting with the Corona rancher, Mack Brazel, and his subsequent call to the airbase near Roswell about the strange wreckage that Brazel had brought to town.[9] The book was based upon interviews of 93 people conducted during the 1978–80 time frame, but apparently none of those were with surviving Wilcox family members. (Sheriff Wilcox's wife, Inez, was still alive. She lived until 1988 without ever being interviewed by researchers.)

In 1990, the Roswell research team of Kevin Randle and Don Schmitt interviewed the Wilcox children, daughters Phyllis (McGuire) and Elizabeth (Tulk). They learned that their late father was greatly disappointed—even bitter—with the way the military had handled the 1947 crash, because he felt that he had been cut out of what was going on, even though he had legal jurisdiction over all of the goings-on in his county. He told them that, if he could do it over again, he would have called the press *first* so they could get to the crash sites and get the story out before the military got it and covered it up. As reported in their groundbreaking 1991 book, *UFO Crash at Roswell,* Randle and Schmitt hint at Sheriff Wilcox's key role: "Without his phone call [to the military] the information might have spread farther, faster so that the Army [Air Corps] would not have been able to contain it. With that one phone call, Wilcox helped create a mystery that continues to endure [to this day]."[10]

Although both Wilcox daughters had been in their early 20s and married at the time of the 1947 incident, not as much was learned from them about it as one would have hoped. They did say that their father had wondered why Brazel would have come all the way from Corona to Roswell (a two- to three-hour drive in those days) if he didn't think it (the strange wreckage) was *something*.[11] So he (Sheriff Wilcox) dispatched two deputies to try to locate the Brazel crash site, which they did not reach due to encroaching darkness, but they did find a circular, burned area where the ground had been blackened and baked hard, as if intense heat had been applied to it. The daughters were not sure, but they thought that their father had gone out to the crash site himself but that it was much closer to Roswell than the Brazel site, which was 75 miles from of Roswell, much closer— an apparent second crash site. They did not know, however, when that was (before or after the military had gotten there). They said that their parents had been warned by the military not to say anything but did not expand upon what that meant. When they wanted to learn more about what had happened, they were simply told by their mother, Inez, "Don't ask so many questions."[12] Unfortunately for history, they complied with their mother's wishes.

Fortunately for history, a fellow with the impressive appellation, Prince Hans Adam of Liechtenstein, was interested in the subject of UFOs, and especially the Roswell case. It happens. And in 1991 he funded a "tell-all" that brought two dozen of the key Roswell witnesses to Washington, DC, for the purpose of having their testimonies regarding their involvement in the 1947 incident videotaped for posterity.[13] Among those selected to go to Washington to tell their stories were the Wilcox daughters, Phyllis McGuire and Elizabeth Tulk. Their videotaped accounts did not deviate to any extent from what they had told Randle and Schmitt the year before. Nothing new to see here. Not traveling to Washington, however, even though she had been invited to go, was someone who would "blow the lid off" the extent of the constitutionally illegal behavior by our military back in 1947—the brutish tactics employed to silence civilian witnesses, which up to that point had been kept secret for decades under threats of death.

Barbara Duggar (pronounced "Doo-gaarr") of Dell City, Texas, is the second oldest of three daughters born to Elizabeth and Jay Tulk. Her older sister, Phyllis Anne, passed away in 2013, and her younger sister, Christine, lives in Arizona. The sisters are the granddaughters of George and Inez Wilcox. Now retired, Barbara possesses two Master's Degrees (one in Business Administration and another in Business Education) from Eastern New Mexico University, plus a DEd (Doctor of Education) from New Mexico State University. Starting out as an instructor in Business Administration at New Mexico Military Institute in Roswell in the mid-1970s, she went on to become a secondary school teacher and ultimately rose to the position of Superintendent of Schools for the city of Dell City for many years thereafter.

Barbara had been asked but refused to attend the 1991 confab in Washington because of a conflicted conscience: She had promised her grandmother, Inez Wilcox (whom the family lovingly called "Big Mom"), years before that she would never tell anyone what Inez had revealed to her about what happened to them back in 1947.[14] She eventually relented to be interviewed in her home in time for it to be included in the video documentary resulting from the Washington Roswell witness depositions, *Recollections of Roswell*, but too late for

Randle and Schmitt's *UFO Crash at Roswell* book, which had already gone to press. Barbara was very emotional—on the verge of tears—during most of the videotaped interview. When asked why that was, Barbara said that it was because she realized that she was breaking her vow of silence made many years before to her grandmother Inez never to tell. But her internal struggle ended with her breaking of her self-imposed silence, "If she [Inez] couldn't tell it, I can!"[15]

Barbara was not yet born when the 1947 Roswell crash occurred, and in the fall of 1969 she was about to enter her freshman year of college at Eastern New Mexico University in Roswell. Her own parents lived out of town, so Barbara stayed with her grandmother Inez in Roswell during the school week. By July of that year, Barbara was getting ready for the approaching school year and also getting comfortable at her grandmother's place. Like most other people on the historic day of July 20, 1969, Barbara and her grandmother, Inez "Big Mom" Wilcox, found themselves ensconced in front of the TV set, watching the live broadcast of the first manned, moon landing by America's *Apollo 11* astronauts. At one point in the proceedings, Inez asked her granddaughter, "Barbara, do you believe in anything [life] out in space?" Barbara responded, "You know I do. Why do ask? What is it you want me to know, Big Mom?"[16]

The first moon landing of July 1969 was not only one of the seminal events in human history, it also seemed to have had a cathartic effect upon several Roswell witnesses or surviving family members who, up to that point in time, had kept the secret. We have run into a number of witnesses who have told us that it was seeing the moon landing that made them, a parent, or a grandparent, feel that it was then acceptable for them to talk about the 1947 Roswell events—not all of them, to be sure, but a fair number of them. Such as it apparently was with Inez Wilcox. According to Barbara Duggar, her grandmother then arose from her chair, closed and locked all of the doors, went over to the window, closed it and drew the curtains, sat back down, looked around, and spoke to her in a whisper about the 1947 flying saucer crash near Roswell and, especially, how she and her husband, George, had been treated by the U.S. military back then.[17]

Before starting, Inez made Barbara promise never to tell anyone what she was about to hear—that she had kept it secret and buried within herself since 1947 but now (seeing the moon landing), she just had to tell someone. She told Barbara that a flying saucer had crashed near Roswell in 1947, and that her husband George had gone out to the site, which was located about 30 miles north of Roswell. (Note: This was the final or Impact Site located in Chaves County, not the first or Brazel debris field site located 75 miles north/northwest of Roswell in Lincoln County). There, he saw some metallic wreckage and that "there had been bodies found [three dead and one still alive], little men with big heads wearing gray, silk-like uniforms."[18] (Our research also indicates that there were *two* bodies found dead and one "live one" found walking around at this site.[19])

According to Barbara, Big Mom then related to her that, after things had quieted down a bit from the initial excitement, the military came to the jailhouse again. It was not to thank George for "helping out the boys over at the base."[20] It was to threaten the sheriff, his wife, and the rest of his family if they ever talked to anybody about what had just happened in Roswell. According to Barbara, "If George and Inez ever talked about it in any way, not only would they be killed, but they would get the rest of the family."[21] There was no mention by Barbara of the military's getting physical with George at this time—just verbal threats. But Phyllis McGuire, who was upstairs at the jailhouse that day, saw things a little differently. In a 1990 interview, she related to us that the military had "stormed" the jailhouse that day after they learned that a second box of UFO wreckage that rancher Mack Brazel had brought into town on July 6th had been left at the sheriff's office. Jeeps manned by armed MPs swept up to the jailhouse like an invading army and surrounded it. Her startled father was then accosted by the officer in charge, who grabbed him, swung him around, and shoved him frontally against an office wall, while locking the Sheriff of Chaves County's right arm behind him in a hammer-lock, like a common criminal. *"Okay, where is it?"* Still in the grip of the thug-like officer, George Wilcox shuffled as best he could into one of the side rooms and pointed to a closet near the door with his free left arm. After retrieving the box from the closet, the officer released his grip on the sheriff and marched him like a buck-private back into the main room of the office, where Wilcox's wife, having come down from the upstairs residence to see what all the commotion was about, was waiting. The officer then ordered both George and Inez to sit down, while he remained standing and dictated in no uncertain terms the conditions under which the Wilcox family—parents and children alike—could continue to remain among the extant.[22]

According to our recent interview with Barbara Duggan, she was told by Inez that the military contingent that came into the jailhouse that day was led by a "real tall officer with red hair."[23] He had two of his "goons" with him, as well, and there were military vehicles outside surrounding the jailhouse with MPs sitting in them. All of them had guns. "Did you hear them say that [the threats], Big Mom?" "Yes, Barbara, I did." "Did you believe them?" Big Mom pondered the question for half a nanosecond and responded, "What do you think?"[24]

Inez concluded her account to Barbara by stating that, when it was over, her husband no longer wanted to be sheriff. Whether it was seeing the alien creatures or being threatened by the military, George Wilcox became so upset and demoralized that he never ran for sheriff again. Inez, on the other hand, was so angry at the way they had been treated that she picked up the baton dropped by her husband and ran for the office herself. According to Barbara, Inez ran for sheriff when George declined "just to show *them* that they could not do this to them!"[25] She did not lose by much. "Her opponents ran a smear campaign against her, saying that she and George and the entire family were 'crazy' and so forth." George was a nice man. Everybody loved him, especially the Hispanic community. George could speak Spanish, and he was very close to that community.[26]

Until her "confessional" to Barbara Duggar in 1969, Inez Wilcox's only outlet to relieve some of the built-up angst over what had happened in 1947 was to sit down and write a one-page account of what had taken place—the flying saucer crash and its aftermath, as she knew it—for posterity. The gist of her piece, which still exists today, was that there were still many unanswered questions regarding the crash for which no one was providing answers. She wrote that the only thing that the military ever told them was to never talk about it.[27] According to Barbara, however, that wasn't quite accurate. George and Inez were told by the red-haired officer who had come to the jailhouse to retrieve the second box of Brazel's wreckage that "[t]he American people were not smart enough to handle *this* [the crash of an interstellar craft and crew from another world], and it would be devastating for the country, because it has to rebuild from the war" [authors' emphasis].[28] However, her husband George had seen and handled some of the wreckage himself when Brazel came to his office and had also been to the crash site north of town, where he witnessed additional wreckage and, more importantly, the unearthly little bodies with big heads. More likely, then, George and Inez had wanted to know something definitive regarding the drama in which they had played unwitting roles that they did not audition for—answers that never came.

George Wilcox died a "broken man" in a mental hospital in Las Vegas, New Mexico, in 1961. His wife Inez, until the day she died in 1988, believed that the military had *"snuffed him out,"* because he was never the same after the military got through with him.[29] According to Inez, a few days after the visit by the thuggish, red-haired officer to the sheriff's office at the jailhouse, George was summoned to the airbase (Roswell Army Air Field) for a further, unspecified "discussion." Not knowing what it was about or what to expect, George took two of his deputies along with him, just in case. When he came back from the base, according to Inez, he was acting "very strange." He had a faraway look on his face, and his overall appearance looked as though he had been "roughed up." She said he was never the same after that and felt that the military had given him some sort of injection or something that led to his ultimate demise. "He just went 'crazy' afterwards and didn't want to be sheriff anymore." When Wilcox's older daughter, Phyllis, was asked in an early interview by us as to how the 1947 incident might have affected her father, without hesitating she responded forcefully, *"It destroyed him!"*[30]

George and Inez ultimately moved from Roswell to Dexter, New Mexico, where Inez opened up a small grocery store to help make ends meet. They never discussed the 1947 incident with their family again, until Inez broke her silence about it with her granddaughter in 1969. She had not even spoken to her own daughters, Phyllis (McGuire) and Elizabeth (Tulk), about it since 1947, when she told Phyllis to stop asking questions. And for their part, Phyllis and Elizabeth never talked about it with their own children. When confronted, Elizabeth's husband, Jay, told us that it was all, "Just a crock of s—," to which Elizabeth interjected, "Oh, Jay, you know better than that, because you were there when the MPs were there."[31] He *was* there, but he was obviously trying to deflect questions about it and keep the secret by ridiculing it and, by extension, ridiculing the person asking the questions. However, before he passed away in 1993 at age 69, Jay Tulk obviously had at least a mild change of heart about Roswell. Most likely, this was derived from his wife Elizabeth's participation in the 1991 Roswell witness confab in Washington, DC. After a presentation by Randle and Schmitt in Lovington, New

Mexico, one evening in the early 1990s, Tulk approached Schmitt just to tell him, "Keep on going. You're on the right track."[32] Where had we heard that before? For Jay Tulk, however, that was telling us a lot.

One additional insult foisted upon George Wilcox by the military, perhaps the "final straw" that sent him over the edge, was something never mentioned by any of the surviving family members. Perhaps they did not know. Perhaps they forgot. Perhaps it was too disturbing to bring up. Barbara Duggar told us that it was entirely unknown to her prior to being interviewed for this book, as neither Inez ever mentioned it to her back in 1969, nor had any other family members since.[33] Whether he simply just rolled over in the face of a military "full-court press" or simply felt that, because the airbase south of town contributed so much to the economic well-being of the town of Roswell, he'd better accede to their wishes, the military enlisted Sheriff Wilcox to silence local civilians who knew too much about the incident, especially those who had seen or even knew about the bodies.[34] And because he could speak Spanish fluently, he was on point for delivering the vicious "silence or death" threats to the Hispanic community in Roswell (e.g., the Anaya family members; see Chapter 2). This would have been totally out of character for the easygoing sheriff, and it appears that he was just totally overwhelmed by the incident and its aftermath, so much so that he had to get away from it all after it was over. There is no record or hint that George ever spoke again about it, and Inez only spoke that one time—to her granddaughter in 1969—when she couldn't keep it in any longer. When she was finished, her granddaughter asked if she was still afraid, to which Big Mom replied, a resounding "Yes!"[35]

As for Barbara Duggar and her sisters, they all appear to have led exemplary lives of achievement, unaffected by the 1947 incident and the secrets kept so long by her parents and grandparents. However, taking it all in, Barbara concluded, "It was horrifying for my family,"[36] meaning her parents and grandparents, as Barbara and her sister Christine were not born until after the incident and were not made aware of it until much later. Barbara was interviewed one time, for the 1992 documentary *Recollections of Roswell*, after which she said she received a spate of letters, which she answered. But she never spoke about Roswell again until being interviewed by us for this book. FOX TV even called her for an on-camera interview, but she told them in no uncertain terms, *"Absolutely not!"*[37]

George McGuire, now 72 years old, is the oldest of four children born to Phyllis and Ralph McGuire, as well as the oldest grandchild of George and Inez Wilcox. Contacted by us in July 2015 for this book, he had never before been interviewed by anyone regarding the 1947 Roswell events. Now a retired air traffic controller, he was "there" in Phoenix, Arizona, at the time of the famous "Phoenix Lights" UFO incident in 1996.[38] His mother, Phyllis, who died in 2008 at the age of 85, and his father, Ralph, who died in 2012 at the age of 92, divorced in 1978. He revealed to us that ever since he was a little kid, before he ever heard of the Roswell Incident and his family's role in it, he "was 'scared' of UFOs," but didn't know why. He still can't explain it. Perhaps it stemmed from a day in July of 1947 when he was at a jail-house in Roswell with his mother and a military officer with the red-hair came-by. He was only 4 years old, but maybe it was one of those unpleasant memories suppressed and buried deeply in the psyche of a small child—never quite remembered, but never totally forgotten.

George McGuire told us that most of what he knows about the 1947 incident he got from his mother. But he was quick to add that the Tulk daughters, Barbara and Christine, know much more about it than he. He said that he first became interested in it when his mother and aunt went to Washington in 1991 to tell what they knew. "It was only after my mother and my aunt Elizabeth went to Washington and investigators starting coming around that I started asking questions. Prior to that, it was kind of a hush-hush thing." After that, he said that he had a few discussions with his mother Phyllis, but that was the extent of his interest.

We have learned from experience that, whenever a witness tells you that you or someone else probably knows more about it (the subject matter of the interview) than he or she does, you should still conduct a full interview of that person, because a "nugget" or two that you did not know before almost always turns up. And so it was with George McGuire.

Beginning in 1958, when 15-year-old George McGuire was a student at NMMI (New Mexico Military Institute) in Roswell, he got to spend a lot of time with his Wilcox grandparents, especially George. The 1947 incident was never talked about, according to McGuire, be he knew there was something wrong with the former sheriff. Aware that his grandfather never worked again after the incident, he recalled, "I was curious, but I never asked him about it." Reflecting now, after so many years, "He was paranoid and was always scared that somebody was after him. Whenever a car went by, he would jump up and look out the window, as if he didn't feel safe. Everything seemed to bother him. One day, he physically attacked my grandmother. That's when they put him in the mental hospital in Las Vegas [NM], where he died a few months later."

In George McGuire's opinion, *something* happened to his grandfather: "I've always had a gut belief that somebody [an organization] or some person threatened my grandfather [so badly that it sent him over the edge]. There's no other explanation for the way he acted." Was it just the Alzheimer's or *something* that triggered its early onset that inexorably ended with Sheriff George Wilcox's death 14 years after the 1947 incident? To watch his deterioration must have been horrifying for the family, because it seemed to have occurred overnight. No one knew him better than his wife, Inez, and she believed to her dying day that her husband's life had been cut short (i.e., "snuffed out") like that of a common criminal, simply for "helping out the boys over at the base."

CHAPTER 4

"Take You Out Into the Desert, and They'll Never Find You"

Walter Haut graciously allowed us the use of his home in 1991 to participate in a radio interview with radio legend Larry Glick of WHDH in Boston. While Don Schmitt fielded questions from one phone in the Haut home office, Frankie Rowe of Portales, New Mexico, listened in from another phone in the front room until she would join the live-broadcast discussion. Frankie had not been interviewed on the radio before, and there appeared to be some stage fright as a direct question to her was met with total silence. But the dead air continued, then was replaced by sobbing. From Schmitt's phone it sounded as though Frankie was crying in the background.

The host of the program, Glick, immediately turned off the live feed from their phone line and broke for a commercial as Schmitt urgently raced into the other room. There, Frankie was weeping, cupping her face with both hands as she exhorted, "That

Frankie Dwyer Rowe was threatened by a military officer to remain silent about what she had seen and heard from her father in 1947, or she and her family would meet their demise out in the desert. Photo from 2010.

85

voice…that accent…that's exactly how that man sounded. That's how the man who came into our house sounded." She wasn't able to continue. Glick, who was born in Massachusetts and had a Boston accent, immediately understood. Another man with the same inflection in his voice had left a haunting threat, which lasted 45 years. Frankie Dwyer Rowe would never forget.[1]

We know of several instances when military authorities took matters into their own hands by employing thuggish tactics directly to a civilian eyewitness to scare them into silence. Perhaps they thought they could get away with it because the witnesses couldn't defend themselves. Perhaps they needed to make sure that everything was contained as they assessed the entire situation. Frankie Dwyer was a 12-year-old schoolgirl in July 1947, and her encounter with the bullying and threatening military officer haunts her to this day. Frankie's father was a crew chief with the Roswell Fire Department. At the time of the incident, Frankie had just been to the dentist and had stopped at the fire station to wait for her father to take her home. While she was waiting, a state highway patrol officer by the name of Robert Scroggins stopped by the firehouse. Scroggins lived southeast of Roswell in the town of Hobbs, but this time he had a special reason for going out of his way for stopping in town.

After he called his friends to gather, he reached into his pocket and took out *something* that he held out in his hand. Next, he crumbled up the thin piece of what looked like some sort of foil. He then held his hand back out over a nearby table and released his grip, as the piece of metal-like material dropped to the surface without making a sound. Then, as if by magic, it spread out like "quicksilver" into a perfectly smooth piece of paper-thin material in just a matter of seconds. Everyone there took turns handling and examining the "magic" piece, including Frankie Dwyer. She described how it "flowed like water" each and every time she crushed it, then dropped it to the floor of the fire house. They all observed that it couldn't be cut with a knife, scratched, burned by a cigarette lighter, or permanently creased. No one had any idea what or where it was from. All Officer Scroggins would admit was that he acquired the piece from "someone up in Corona." He retrieved the piece and said he needed to show it to someone else in town.[2]

A day or two later, Frankie was at home with her mother helping around the house when there was a hard knock at the kitchen door. Mrs. Dwyer opened the entrance to greet someone who she never expected. There was a tall man with broad shoulders and ruddy complexion in a MP uniform, and he was looking for her daughter. The woman was caught completely off guard and at first didn't know how to answer. "I have two daughters," she nervously responded. "You have a daughter named Frankie," he stated. After Mrs. Dwyer introduced her daughter to the ominous MP, two other MPs escorted her mother into another room. With a heavy New York accent, the officer started to question Frankie about the incident at the fire station and wanted to know exactly all that she had seen—including who else was there. Satisfied that the 12-year-old had seen too much, he drew his billy club out from its holster and proceeded to pound the shaft into his open palm. And with each new warning he pounded the club harder and harder. "You did not see anything. Do you understand? If you say anything, not only will you be killed, but we will come back for your family. There's a big desert out there. No one will ever find you." With that, a shaken Mrs. Dwyer was returned to her terrified daughter, and the men left.[3]

In researching Frankie Dwyer Rowe's story over the years, we followed the evidence trail to conclude that the MP who most likely confronted young Frankie that day was a former Brooklyn, New York, policeman by the name of Arthur Philbin, who was a security officer with the 390th Air Service Squadron (ASS) that was part of the Roswell Army Air Field (RAAF)'s 509th Bomb group in 1947.

Lieutenant Philbin, in addition to being 6 foot 4 inches tall and built like an NFL lineman, ran the guard house on the base and had also

served as a security liaison with the Roswell local police and sheriff's department. Whenever base activities extended into the town of Roswell, Philbin coordinated all the necessary security. Philbin passed away in 1970 at the age of 50, so it was impossible to hear his account of the events, which apparently extended his jurisdiction into the homes of civilians back in 1947. Therefore, we had never published anything about the man or anything that mentioned his name. We also never mentioned his name to Frankie Dwyer Rowe.

Lt. Arthur Philbin was identified by Frankie Rowe as the intimidating Army officer who had threatened her back in 1947.

In 2005, we had an idea. Why not try a lineup similar to what police do when they parade a number of people in a group that includes the suspect before the witness? The witness has an opportunity to select, without influence, the suspect from the rest of the group. We already had a photograph of Lieutenant Philbin in the 1947 RAAF yearbook. He is shown on page 90 along with the pictures of 16 other officers— enough for an unbiased lineup by any standard. We made a photocopy of the pertinent page from the yearbook and sent it to Frankie Dwyer Rowe with the simple question "Do you recognize anyone on the enclosed page as the person who came to your home and threatened you back in 1947?" A few weeks later, we received an envelope in the mail bearing Frankie Rowe's return address. Inside the envelope was the folded, photocopied page that we had originally sent to her. There was no accompanying letter or note, just the page with the pictures of the 17 officers of the 390th ASS on it. There was a single circle drawn around the photograph of Arthur Philbin.[4]

When the initial call came into the Roswell Fire Station about a downed aircraft north of town, before they could even respond, a colonel from the RAAF arrived on the scene. He quickly informed those on duty that "an unknown object from someplace else" had crashed. He instructed them that they were not to discuss the incident and that the military would handle it. But as previously believed, it wasn't the fire department that made a run out to the crash but rather crew chief Dan Dwyer along with companion Lee Reeves, in his personal car. Arriving before the army could secure the site, Dwyer and Reeves were able to get close enough to the scene. All the talk back in town was true: "From someplace else" was putting it mildly. It wasn't an airplane but an egg-shaped vessel of some sort that they did not recognize. They also observed two or three bodies lying in the lee of the craft. They were about the size of a 10-year-old child, "but they weren't human!"[5]

There were some pieces of wreckage scattered about and, as they scanned the countryside, out of the corner of Dwyer's eye he witnessed the unimaginable. There, staggering off to the side was "a live one," which resembled the others.[6] It appeared to be uninjured yet seemed to be struggling in the aftermath of the crash.

Within moments, the roar of approaching engines filled the landscape and the next thing the two firefighters heard was the shouting of men and MPs who quickly approached them with rifles drawn. They were shuffled off site, an officer warned them of the consequences of repeating a word of the rapidly changing situation, and they were permitted to leave. Getting back into Dwyer's car, the two firefighters hurriedly returned to the fire station. Would anyone believe them? The threat of repercussions gave them an out. They said nothing.[7]

Known as the "Iron Major," the Roswell city manager was a decorated WWII vet of the only independent tank battalion in the Mediterranean Theater of Operations to receive the President's Unit Citation. C.M. Woodbury was a member of the 752nd Tank Battalion, which had experienced some of the most difficult combat of the war in the Battle for Bologna during the Italian Campaign. He was also a good personal friend of the RAAF commander, Colonel William H. "Butch" Blanchard. A short time after Dwyer and Reeves arrived back at the fire station, a most intimidating figure walked in to confront the men. "You are not to say another word about the crash," sternly warned Woodbury. That same evening, after the city manager sat down to dinner with his wife he instructed her in a similar manner, "Don't ever ask me about the incident again."[8]

Still later, Dan Dwyer would arrive home a little past his usual time. Frankie would overhear the private discussion between her parents while standing near her bedroom doorway. She heard a cursory account of what took place that afternoon and the threatening remarks about not discussing the truth of the matter. According to her older sister, Helen, what their mother next told their father incensed him. Helen Cahill was married and living in California in 1947, and recalled how angry her father was about the menacing visitors who entered their home earlier that evening. She confirmed that something important had happened, and that her father would not tell her anything about what he saw. Her mother, however, said that the family would be in trouble if their father ever spoke out about his involvement. "You are better off if you don't know," her father would always remind her.[9]

In as much that the Dwyer family surely knew otherwise, there remained few others in the community to risk speaking with. One change was sadly evident: Prior to the incident, the relationship between the city of Roswell and the personnel stationed south of town couldn't have been more congenial. Many of the officers and other recruits lived off-base and shared streets and neighborhoods with native Roswellians. There was a mutual respect and trust especially coming off the victory of WWII. These were acknowledged heroes who were not only welcome, but served as the best in America as roll-models for the civilian children. The RAAF became synonymous with all that was good in the United States. That was until the Incident.

The military killed more than the story of the millennium on July 8, 1947. They killed off that exemplary relationship shared by both the men and women sworn to defend and protect their families, their neighbors, every breathing soul in this land of the free, and those very people who placed their heads on their pillows each night confident that they were safe and protected. After that time, the people of Roswell lived in suspicion and distrust. Everyone was a potential informer. Everyone had a price. And the military base was now looked upon with jaundiced eyes and cynicism. How could anyone trust them when that faith, which welcomed them into the community, was now replaced with spite and distain—and all over a silly balloon. Needless to say, it was because every participant, who in truth knew that they had been forced to live a lie, only embittered themselves all the more toward their enforcers. Dan Dwyer and his family were destined to remain on the shortlist of those enforcers. And so, if you wanted to remain safe, you complied. If you wanted to protect your family as Dan Dwyer, you kept silent. Fear is a tremendous motivator.[10]

Just a week before the wedding of Frankie's younger sister, Anice Sue (Suzie), and Ken Letcher in March 1959 something unforeseen took place. Ken had only lived in Roswell for the previous six years and had no prior knowledge of how 1947 specifically affected his soon-to-be new family. His future father-in-law was about to take a chance he hadn't in almost a dozen years. It was after a family dinner party that Dan and Ken went for an early evening walk on a brisk star-lit March evening. It was as though Dan knew that he would only have this one opportunity.

After the standard father-son-in-law type of chat, Dan quickly shifted gears by bringing up 1947. Ken, who was just 8 years old at the time of the incident, expressed only vague memories of what had happened back then. "Wasn't that just a balloon?" Ken innocently commented. And then, an entirely different attitude overcame Dan. His mannerism became fidgety and nervous, and he started to glance in all directions. "Did my daughter ever say anything about back then?" queried Dan. When Ken answered that she had not, Dan started to paint the same scenario that he had only shared with his wife and, albeit briefly, Frankie. "It's all true. I saw it myself and since that time I can't risk saying too much. They even shut up the sheriff, and he was out there too," confessed Dan. "Balloon? That's what the people want to believe. But those of us who were out there saw the wreckage and those bodies—those bodies, which weren't from here," added Dan.[11]

Ken was dumbfounded. What was he getting himself into by marrying into a family that saw UFOs and little men from outer space? But the middle-aged man was more than sincere; he was downright afraid. "Why can't you talk about this? If it's all true, shouldn't we know about it?" asked Ken. "You have to promise me. You have to swear. If my daughter means anything to you. Don't ever say a word. Not even to my family," pleaded Dan.

On March 8, 1959, Dan walked Suzie up the aisle of St. Peter 's Catholic Church. The ceremony took place on a bright, sunny, late winter's day in Roswell. Dan seemed very content and enjoyed himself throughout the festive affair. Four days later, Ken left to serve in the U.S. Army. As though he had a premonition, human affairs continued to move quickly as Dan would drop to the floor from a massive heart attack at the young age of 55. As the news arrived, all Ken could do was send a wire message making sure his new bride was okay. The words about 1947 weighed especially heavy that night.

When Frankie married James E. Rowe and moved to Portales, New Mexico, with her new husband, thoughts of Roswell and all those fearful times could be left behind her. Now that her father was gone, it became a subject that her mother and sister considered off limits, as the pain became resentment, which was often directed at the easiest target: Frankie. The move to another city enabled her to put some well-needed distance from 1947, but not for everyone.

Frankie Dwyer Rowe's name remained on the "watch list" not only for those witnesses remaining in Roswell since 1947, but also outsiders monitoring the situation. When we arrived in New Mexico to start our own independent investigation of the incident, within short order we were introduced to Frankie and met with her at her home. To this day she remains one of our premiere witnesses and, sadly, one of the few remaining survivors. Somewhere, someone has a "scratch sheet" where they continue to cross off the names. We remain fortunate that they will have to continue waiting for Frankie Rowe.

In 1997, not long after all the festivities in Roswell commemorating the 50th anniversary of the event, a bad wind storm hit the area including Portales, which is an hour northeast of Roswell. Along with others, the Rowes lost phone service due to downed phone wires, and a Quest technician would have to make repairs. His last duty was to check the phone box that fed the outside line into the house. Opening the metal box, he could have just as well encountered a snake. But in Frankie's case, the past was about to rear a figurative snake's head. The confused repairman rapped on the door, which Frankie opened. "Mrs. Rowe, I don't know if you are aware that someone has placed a wiretap on your phone line," the man amusingly informed her. Frankie was totally dumbfounded and all those past fears came rushing back like the storm that had just blown through town. "I want it off right now," demanded Frankie, but the considerate man had already performed the service. "Here it is," handing it to her. "I'm sure it's not legal, and I know it's nothing we install. In fact, I've never seen anything like it before."[12] Not exactly the type of souvenir that increases one's faith in their government.

Wiretapping phone device that a technician discovered in the telephone box of Frankie Rowe's home in 1997.

The next time we met with Frankie, she turned over the device to us and we immediately had the late Chester Lytle, Sr., president of Communications Diversified of Albuquerque, examine the wire instrument. Quickly he identified it as a "listening device" manu-factured by Motorola back in the Fifties. Lytle had worked as an engineering designer for both Motorola and Zenith during that time. "Someone is monitoring the phone calls of your friend," stated Lytle.[13] It was too bad they hadn't left a calling card or a tag reading, "For service contact your friendly neighborhood government agent, John Smith at...." More impor-tantly, with no infractions on either Frankie or her husband's record or nothing else of concern in their backgrounds—that is, except for Frankie, who was now publicly speaking out about Roswell, we were slightly amused, whereas Frankie and James were upset and angry. The harassment of the children of Roswell continued long into their adulthood. We had physical proof, but we were frustrated that we couldn't trace the intruding line back to its source. To our knowledge, no one has ever replaced the device, so Mother Nature's storm provided us with quite a revelation.

Two years later, James would pass away, and within a few more years, Frankie decided to go home—back to Roswell. She would take a stand for her fallen loved ones, for all the children of Roswell, raised in a free nation, raised to see suppression and fear of the very government sworn to protect that freedom. For the next 10 years Frankie would publicly speak out the truth about what officials of that government sadly did to her family. But the greatest surprise came with a single phone call in the early fall of 2012.

The male caller introduced himself as Brian, and that he would like to stop by in Roswell while passing through the state. He explained that he had something he wanted to give her, and much to Frankie's shock, she invited him to stop by her house. Frankie had never remarried and lived alone west of town on a rural stretch of road. After all these years, she was now inviting a total stranger in to see her? But "Brian" sounded sincere, and his voice actually sounded genuine, as though he, too, had a story to tell.

The doorbell rang, and Frankie had an immediate flashback to that day back in 1947 when that ominous man with the Brooklyn accent came to their home.[14] "Frankie Rowe, my name is Brian Philbin. I'm the son of Arthur Philbin—the man who threatened you all those years back. He died more than 40 years ago, but he would want me to give you these," he said as he presented her with a large bouquet of flowers. "He would want me to say that he was sorry, that he was just following orders at that time." Frankie was completely speechless.[15] She took the flowers and tearfully accepted the apology. And with that response, a hundred restless ghosts from 1947 also accepted the apology. For the first time in many years, Frankie Rowe contemplated all the pain which had befallen her family, and smiled.

CHAPTER 5

The Families Remember—The Ghosts Remain Silent

"**C**ome on, Brownie. Let's have a look inside," came the retort from his boss outside of the "big hangar," as it was often called.

Sergeant Melvin E. Brown was a cook in the 509th Bomb Group in 1947 who had a Top Secret security clearance. He accompanied the dead alien bodies from the Impact Site back to the Roswell base. Told not to look under the covering tarp, he did, and he lived to later tell about it.

Sergeant Melvin E. Brown stepped inside with his boss, Captain John R. Martin, commanding officer of the Roswell Army Air Field (RAAF) Squadron K. There was only a wooden crate resting on the floor of P-3, one of two B-29 hangars on the base. Brown informed the officer that the crate was packed and sealed for shipment to Fort Worth. That's all Brown could tell Martin, so they walked outside and he resumed his post. Within the next few months, "Brownie" was transferred to the United Kingdom, met his future bride, Ada, and made his new home in England.[1]

It was on the occasion of America's first manned landing on the moon in July 1969 that Brown told his family the story of Roswell. His daughter Beverly

J. Bean described the conversation: "In 1969, he told my sister and me that he was ordered to go out into the desert. He said that all available men were grabbed to go out to where a crashed saucer had come down…and there were several bodies."[2] Much to the consternation of the loyal former military man, his two daughters, Beverly and Harriet, laughed off his wild tale of witnessing a flying saucer crash 20 years before. Despite their reluctance to believe him, Brown emphasized that none of them should utter a word because "Daddy will get into trouble."

While on his deathbed in 1986 at a hospital just outside of London, his daughter Beverly described a father now distraught over the notion that the world believed that all that crashed outside of Roswell in 1947 was something that it wasn't.

"It was not a damn weather balloon," he groaned over and over again tossing and turning in his bed. "For the last couple of days of his life, all he talked about was Roswell," recounted his daughter sadly.

What Melvin Brown had divulged to his loved ones back in 1969 was the following: It was about dusk when Brown had completed his normal duty assignments, when he was dispatched to accompany a number of select men from other units into the desert. Once there, he and one other soldier were stationed in the cargo area of one of the ambulance trucks.

"I couldn't understand why ice was being loaded into some of the waiting trucks. What did they need to keep cold?" Once boarded, they were ordered not to look under a tarp bunched up in a pile between them. Just as soon as the vehicle lumbered away from the remote base of operation, the two guards pulled back the canvas cover—and their lives changed in that instant.

Brown described them to his family as smaller than human. There were two of them. The scuttle back at the base was true. With far-from-adequate lighting in the truck, the color and texture of the skin looked strange: "They had big heads with slanted eyes."[3]

Now, while he was dying, he provided his family specific details of a secret bank account back in Roswell that was set up to insure his silence for all those years. They listened attentively as he spelled out an agreement in which specific men were essentially paid hush money—$10,000, no less—complete with an account number.[4] Unfortunately for the Brown survivors, no such account number or name of beneficiaries, no matter which bank we checked with in Roswell, matched. Either the family had the wrong number or no such monetary payoff was ever established. Nonetheless, such a promise did its job.

Beverly remains especially outspokenly upset. Not for the squandered windfall, but, to her much more importantly, the way her father was treated for all of his cooperation and allegiance to a military that withheld the truth about the crash. She becomes especially offended when she sees skeptics on television portray he father and other personnel at Roswell so incompetent as not being able to tell the difference between balloon debris and something truly extraordinary.

"Everyone at that base in Roswell had a Top Security clearance, and it wasn't because they had a habit of seeing things," she sternly added.[5]

Brown's widow, Ada, and oldest daughter, Harriet, still refuse to talk about the 1947 event because they feel it would reflect negatively on his stellar military career. More realistically, their concern is that the Army would retaliate against them. Still, Ada would reflect on those last days before Melvin's passing. She still became emotional at the time we spoke with her last.

"We had said our goodbyes, and then he took me by the hand," she described. "Dear, I want you to know that I have always been faithful to you," her fading husband assured her. And then, as if to equate that warm sentiment with the same level of importance in his life, "He then went on and on about it not being a weather balloon," Ada remarked, still wiping tears from her eyes.[6] Is it any wonder that daughter Beverly takes the abusive treatment of her late father so personally?

Numerous flights had transported hardware from Roswell. In the case of Captain Oliver W. "Pappy" Henderson, he flew a C-54 load of wreckage directly to Wright Field. At Roswell, he was in charge of the "Green Hornet Airline," which also flew C-47s. They specialized in flying dignitaries and materials to the South Pacific during all of the atomic testing. Henderson had also received two Distinguished Flying Crosses and the Air Medal with Four Oak Leaf Clusters for flying 30 missions over Germany during WWII. He kept one special flight a secret from everyone including his wife, Sappho, until the early 1980s.

Henderson, who passed away on March 25, 1986, told his wife that he had wanted to tell her about it for years. He knew that flying saucers were real because he had flown a planeload of wreckage from Roswell on to Wright Field. He didn't tell her much about it except that the debris was strange. The flight's destination had been Dayton, Ohio, and back again in a C-54 transport plane.

Pappy Henderson was a member of the First Air Transport Unit, which was assigned to the Roswell Army Air Field. He would describe to his wife that it was a routine flight except for its high classification status. He never broke his silence about his own role until the last few years before his death.[7]

As has been demonstrated numerous times with those who possess military secrets, the last ones they confide in are their immediate families. Often the many threats to Roswell participants included their families. There is little wonder that they would preserve their innocence at every cost. This does not necessarily apply to trusted friends or confidants. In Henderson's case, it was his close friend and fellow retired military officer Dr. John Kromschroeder, whom he first informed about "transporting spacecraft garbage" to Wright Field. He then shocked his friend by claiming to have also flown "small beings"[8] on the same plane. Henderson morbidly added, "The passengers [of the crash] suffered their death." But the biggest secret was yet to come, for a year later "Pappy" displayed a piece of what he said was actual debris from the crash to his friend—and it was unlike anything Kromschroeder had seen before.

The metal-like artifact was gray and resembled aluminum, but harder and stiffer. Kromschroeder couldn't bend it but had to be careful because the edges were rather sharp. He added that it didn't seem to have a crystalline structure, and based that on the fracturing of it. It hadn't been torn.

Kromschroeder said that Henderson told him that the metal was part of the lighter material lining the interior of the craft. He said that when properly energized, it produced a perfect illumination and cast a soft light with no shadow.

According to Kromschroeder, the piece was retrieved soon thereafter by "someone from Washington," who also reminded him of his security oath. Still, it remained difficult for the retired officer to not hint at what he knew to be the truth.

Henderson's wife Sappho remembered that while they still lived in Roswell, her husband had been outside with Mary Katherine, their daughter, staring into the night sky. When asked what he was doing, he told her, "Looking for flying saucers. They're real, you know."[9] The amazing part of Henderson's account was not yet known by anyone in his family—that of flying some of the bodies to Wright Field along with the "strange material."

In 1981, while their daughter was visiting their home in Roswell, Mary Katherine's father would finally confess that he knew for a fact that they were "real," because he had seen the bodies from the UFO rumored to have crashed when he was stationed there back in the

Forties. He described them as "...small and pale, with slanted eyes and large heads. They were humanoid-looking, but different from us." He thought there were three bodies and they were clothed in a "strange kind of material."[10]

John G. Tiffany reported that his father was stationed at the base and that his unit, as part of their assignment, supported the 509th Bomb Group in Roswell. According to Tiffany, his father had been sent to a destination in Texas.[11] There they picked up metallic debris and a large cylinder that reminded him of a giant thermos bottle.

Tiffany said the metal was very lightweight and very tough. It was smooth with a glasslike surface, and every attempt the flight crew made to mark it, bend it, or break it failed.

But what bothered the airmen were the unusual cylinder and its unknown contents. Tiffany wasn't sure if his father had actually seen anything resembling bodies, but he did state that two of the corpses were intact. After the flight, the crew felt that they were somehow "contaminated." They couldn't "get over handling something that foreign."

Once they arrived at Wright Field, everything was off-loaded, including the giant capsule. The entire cargo was loaded into trucks, and once the vehicles departed, the flight crew was debriefed by a high-ranking official who told them the flight had never taken place.

Throughout the course of our investigation, one name had stood out among many others: the provost marshal at the RAAF, Major Edwin Easley. Military witnesses describe his involvement at the impact site north of town, Hangar P3, debriefing personnel and warning them about speaking out of turn, and issuing specific orders concerning activities pertaining to the recovery operation, which took place on numerous fronts. Easley would retire a lieutenant colonel and no matter how often his family tried to get him to talk about something they knew him to be thoroughly involved in, he always declined reciting to them the very same remark he made repeatedly to researcher Kevin D. Randle: "I can't talk about it. I'm still sworn to secrecy."[12]

Two years later, in 1992, the lieutenant colonel was undergoing futile attempts to prolong his life after being diagnosed with stage-four stomach cancer. While resting in his bed at Parkland Hospital in Dallas, Texas, he was in the company of his two daughters and his granddaughter. From out of nowhere, the little girl held a present up to the dying Air Force officer. Glancing at it, he made the most revealing remark he had ever said to any of them regarding his lifetime secrecy oath. For one brief moment he entrusted his family with a truth he had shielded them from for more than 40 years. According to his family and Dr. Harold Granick, Easley was totally lucid when he reacted to the gift, "Oh! The creatures!" What his granddaughter brought him was a book: *UFO Crash at Roswell* by Kevin Randle and Donald Schmitt. It took the innocence of a child to crack a rigid wall of silence—and Easley seemed relieved.[13]

Daughter Nancy Strickland, a practicing attorney in the state of Texas, provided us with two documents, one of which confirms her father's position of being bond to his security oath and the other a letter. On August 7, 1990, Roswell researcher Stanton Friedman had mailed Easley a package of material to his home in Fort Worth, Texas. Nancy gave us the intact envelope, never opened by her father. On the outside he wrote, *This is information on the 1947 incident North of Roswell, New Mexico AFB. Being sworn to secrecy I could not and did not give away information to this investigator. This case was presented on T.V. Unsolved Mysteries in September 1989. E.* That particular episode of NBC's *Unsolved Mysteries* presented a very pro-Roswell theme and included Sappho Henderson's account of her husband, "Pappy." Easley never indicated to his family any concerns about how the TV show presented the case.

The other form of suggestive documentation came in the form of a letter of commendation from no less than the Treasury

Department of the United States—specifically the Secret Service. We have received testimony in the past about two specific Treasury agents from Washington, DC, who were assigned by the president to oversee the entire operation during the recovery at Roswell. In fact, one of the men who was named has been confirmed to have served President Truman in 1947. What the letter thanked Easley for was the level of cooperation he was to their department during that special "incident" during that year. No other specifics. No details of which event. There were no visits from the president or vice president to Roswell that year, and no former commanders-in-chief strolled through town. In fact, there are no logged exercises involving the secret service during any part of 1947 in Roswell—except for that special "incident." After Easley made that stunning remark at the hospital, besides voicing his everlasting regret at never being able to talk to his family about Roswell, he explained that the president had asked him "never to speak about the incident again."[14] He kept his word, as he would die within the month.

After the *Unsolved Mysteries* broadcast of September 1989, a former cancer ward nurse from the St. Petersburg Hospital in St. Petersburg, Florida, came forward to describe the final testimony she personally heard form one of her elderly patients. The nurse was Mary Ann Gardner, who worked at the hospital from 1976 to 1977. The patient, a woman whose name Gardner couldn't recall, had been alone in the hospital. Feeling concern for her because she had no visitors, Gardner spent as much time as she could listening to the woman's stories—especially the one about the crashed ship and the "little men" she claimed to have seen.[15]

According to Gardner, "Basically...they had stumbled upon a spaceship of some kind and...there were bodies on the ground... little people with large heads and large eyes. Then the Army showed up and chased them away. The Army people were everywhere and told them that if they ever told anything about it, that the government could always find them."

The dying woman explained that she had been with a team of archaeologists and "was not supposed to be there." We found this specific comment rather intriguing, as, post–WWII, male students would often invite lady friends to accompany them out in the field. To us, this suggested a certain degree of authenticity. The woman continued that the team had been "hunting rocks and looking for fossils. She had gone with a friend." Gardner said the woman was still frightened about official retaliation and soon had nothing more to say about the incident.

"The woman kept looking around as if she was frightened about something and said to me, 'They said they could always find us, so I'd better not say any more.'" Gardner then asked her, "Who? Who can find you after all these years? The woman then answered in a low, wary voice, "The government." Within days, she expired.

After being contacted by Gardner, our first concern was attempting to establish who this woman was. After contacting the hospital, now Humana, and receiving assurances from the administrator that it would search its records of deceased cancer patients from that time period, the plan was that Gardner may then remember the name. Co-author Don Schmitt made the trip down to Florida and was informed by the same administrator that they had changed their minds and would not release any files—files that, according to Florida statute, were defined as public records to be made accessible to the public. We had anticipated such a denial, and after citing that very law, Schmitt was told to take it up with their attorney. Under time constants, Schmitt spent an entire day perusing micro-film of obituary columns from the time in question and returned home with a half-dozen possibilities. Anxious to run them past Gardner, he immediately called her. Whereas before she was fully cooperative and quite curious herself to discover who her source was, she was then belligerent and completely hostile regarding further contact. She noted that it was no longer safe to talk and that, if Schmitt ever called again, "I will call the police."[16] Even more shocking was the fact that she had previously allowed us to interview her on videotape but now was threatening us.

In the years since Mrs. Gardner first came forward with her story, and St. Petersburg/Humana Hospital violated Florida state law by denying Schmitt's request for access to its records, co-author Tom Carey decided to research the anthropological and archaeological literature in an attempt to try to identify Gardner's dying archaeologist. He was able to identify a female archaeologist, who would have been about the right age, who had passed away in 1976 in St. Petersburg, Florida and was one of the names Schmitt tried to have Gardner verify.[17] Since our last conversation her phone number has been unlisted, and numerous letters to her unreturned, unanswered.

At around 3:00 p.m. MST on Wednesday, July 9, 1947, a flight crew from the 393 bomb squadron was shooting on the skeet range at the RAAF. Unexpectedly, they were alerted to prepare for an unscheduled flight. Their operations officer, Major Edgar R. Skelley, ordered the aircraft command pilot, Captain Frederick Ewing, to assemble the entire crew for briefing and preflight. Skelley informed them that they had an immediate flight to and from Fort Worth, Texas. They would not be using their normally assigned aircraft, and they were essentially to "keep their mouths shut throughout the assignment."

Members of the flight crew hastily prepared the specially assigned B-29 Bomber, tail number 7301, the *Straight Flush*, for this clandestine flight. The crew, comprised of Ewing, copilot Lieutenant Edgar Izard, engineer Lieutenant Elmer Landry, navigator James Eubanks, bombardier Lieutenant Felix Martucci, as well as Technical Sergeant Arthur Osepchook, Sergeant Robert Slusher, Sergeant Lloyd Thompson, and Corporal Thaddeus Love quietly spoke among themselves about the mysterious nature of the flight.

Osepchook would later describe to us that Ewing shouted over the radio that they should all "keep [their] mouths shut!" Next, the mission became even stranger: Instead of taxi-ing to the mile-long runways unique to the heavy bombers, Ewing steered the plane out to the west side of the tarmac and slowly maneuvered directly over one of the atomic bomb pits: "Bomb Pit Number 1."

The Silverplate B-29 Bomber Straight Flush *was used to ferry several dead aliens in a large wooden crate from Roswell to Fort Worth, Texas. Photo from the 1940s.*

Strangely, the bomb site was under heavy armed guard, and the only unobstructed areas overseeing the pit were the air traffic tower and the immediate flight line. A sealed, unmarked, rectangular wooden crate was waiting to be loaded into the approaching bomb bay. Final destination: Fort Worth Army Air Field, Fort Worth, Texas. (For a full account of this amazing event, see the chapter titled "Boys…We Just Made History" in *Witness to Roswell* by the authors.[18])

Through the ongoing efforts of tracking down key witnesses to this occurrence, we interviewed former crewmen Thompson, Slusher, and Osepchook, spoke to the widows of Eubanks and Love, and had Matucci slam down the phone in our ears. But the one char-

Major Edgar R. Skelley was the operations officer who ordered the crew and the Straight Flush *aircraft to fly alien bodies out of Roswell to Fort Worth Army Air Field on July 9, 1947.*

acter of this story that remained the most intriguing and enigmatic was their boss, Edgar Skelley.

We had discovered Skelley's whereabouts in Riverside, California, in the mid-1990s. When we first phoned him he was totally nondescript and claimed not to remember anything about the 1947 affair, even after running past him a goodly selection of names from his past squadron. (How does one ever forget the name "Thaddeus D. Love"?) None of the names rang a bell, or so he said. A few years later, another call brought the same results, but we were left with an open invitation that if were ever in California, to stop by.[19] That's all we needed to hear.

The year was 2002 and we got Skelley to agree to meet one of us (Don Schmitt). So, in the company of co-author Carey, Denise Marcel, granddaughter of Jesse Marcel, Sr., and Seargent Arn Oldman, formerly of Space Command at Holloman AFB in Alamogordo, New Mexico, we pulled into the Skelley driveway. While the rest of the passengers waited in our rental car, Schmitt approached the front door. After some delay, an older gentleman wearing a bathrobe and slippers answered after numerous doorbell rings. He was an older version of the photograph from the 1947 base yearbook, but the resemblance was clearly there. Schmitt announced, "Hello, Lieutenant Colonel Skelley. My name is Don Schmitt. You were expecting me."

At first the retired officer looked shocked to see Schmitt, but finally he seemed to remember our previous phone conversation and invited him in. "Excuse me while I get dressed," he said as he went to his bedroom. His wife, Anne, immediately took Schmitt by the arm and into the living room. "You have to get him to talk" she pleaded. "I've been trying for years. Every time something about Roswell comes on TV, I ask him again and again to tell me the truth and he says he can't."[20] She quickly showed Schmitt some buried news stories about the case on the coffee table. "I know he knows the truth but you're my last hope," she whispered as her much-older husband approached down the hallway.

"How can I help you, Mr. Schmitt?" asked Skelley.

After another "briefing" on his participation in the Roswell Incident, he asked something that no other witness had ever asked us before: "Why do you need to know?"

"Why is it important to you?" was another query, and Schmitt didn't know if the retired officer was testing him or merely being obtuse.

Schmitt persisted and attempted to turn the discussion around on Skelley. "Why do you have the need to continue your silence for a weather balloon—unless it was something else?" parried Schmitt.

Next, the officer countered with the old "I don't remember" ploy, and Schmitt saw that the subject was not only a raw issue, but that his opponent was becoming more and more defensive—and agitated. Wanting to keep the door open, the investigator backed off, lastly asking for better directions to the highway. Without hesitation, Skelley verbally painted a precise road map, down to distance and time. So much for failing memory.

On the way to the front door, when her husband was out of earshot, Schmitt suggested to Anne that he would have a number of Edgar's former crewman call her and see if they could eventually get to speak with him. Schmitt stepped from the home with her assurance that it was a wonderful idea and she would anxiously wait to hear back from him. "If anyone can pry the truth from him, they can. Good bye, Mr. Schmitt."[21]

No sooner than returning home, we set out to put our plan in action. The first member of Skelley's old unit we had call his wife was Robert Slusher, then residing in Alamogordo, New Mexico. But something had gone awry since our visit with the Skelleys, for Anne would not discuss anything with Slusher. In fact, she was outright hostile toward him.[22] Next, it was up to Schmitt to learn what could still be salvaged from their original game plan.

Needless to say, Anne reacted the very same way to Schmitt as Slusher described she had in his own attempt to talk with her over the phone. More than anything else, she sounded deeply afraid and terribly uneasy talking about the subject. In fact, she wanted nothing more to do with it—quite a change from just a few weeks before when she practically pled with Schmitt to try to get her husband to talk. There would be one last try. Schmitt didn't ask her what her husband said to her after his departure. We knew better: Husbands who don't speak with their wives about matters of national security don't open that Pandora's box.

Rather, Schmitt asked her, "Who did your husband call?"[23]

With some reluctance to respond, she finally admitted, "Well, he made a number of calls discussing your visit."

"Anyone you know of?" pried Schmitt.

"One was from Denver, and that's all I will say. Now please don't ever call here again. I'm sorry," she sternly said and hung up. That would be the last time we would speak with her until her husband passed away later in 2002. One final attempt was made to call his now widow with the hope that all past restrictions may have passed with her husband. We were rudely mistaken.

"I warned you never to call me again. I have nothing to say to you," screamed Mrs. Skelley into the phone as she slammed it down.[24] This (2010) was years after the last conversation and the fear in her voice was quite real. It wasn't anger. It was as though she realized by even talking with us that her life was in jeopardy. She originally hounded her husband time and time again to tell her the truth. Then we entered the picture and her desire to know what we knew intensified. And yet, her abrupt change of heart came not with ridicule, but rather fear. Fear of the unknown is timelessly like that. Clearly, this poor woman received some answers to questions not asked. It remains someone else's fear that the families continue to search for the truth—a truth that remains unspoken. A distant memory that refuses to die.

CHAPTER 6

An Officer and a Gentleman: Jesse Marcel, Jr.

"**W**ake up, Jesse. Wake up, son. Your dad wants to show you something." Coming out of a sound sleep, 11-year-old Jesse Marcel, Jr., tried hard to adjust his eyes to the darkness. He tried even harder to force himself from his bed and follow the silhouette of what he naturally assumed was his father. "Dad, it's after midnight," exclaimed the weary boy. "Just come to the kitchen," instructed the dark figure.

Major Jesse Marcel was the head of intelligence of the most famous unit within the U.S. military in 1947: the 509th Bomb Group, which was the first nuclear squadron in the world. Just a couple of years before, his young son had asked him what an atomic bomb looked like, and his father privately sketched for him a picture of "Fat Man." A moment later he quickly shredded the drawing and dutifully burned the remains with his lighter. "Promise me you won't ever say a word, or you'll get your father in a lot of trouble." Such mutual trust and respect extended their entire lives. And this night was no different with the officer just returning home after he was away on assignment over the previous two days. What new secrets was he about to share this time with his only child, Jesse, who would never have imagined what was waiting for him in their dining room?[1]

Jesse and his wife Viaud had raised their child well; he was destined for both a stellar military career and healer of the sick. After college, he would complete his pre-med undergraduate work at

Louisiana State University at Baton Rouge. Next, he would graduate with his medical degree from the Louisiana School of Medicine in New Orleans in July 1961. Within the year, he joined the U.S. Navy and was assigned to the transport ship USS *Renville* as a flight surgeon. He retired from active duty in July 1971.[2]

Back home, Dr. Marcel would enter private practice in Helena, Montana, and opened his ear, nose, and throat clinic, but he was still drawn to the military. In 1973 he joined the Montana Army National Guard and devoted weekends as a helicopter pilot-instructor and flight surgeon at Fort Rucker in Alabama. He would serve as the State Surgeon for Montana and would retire from the military for a second time in August 1996 with the full rank of Colonel.

As a final testimony to his loyalty and dedication to his country, he was called back to active duty in October 2004—at the age of 68. He served as a flight surgeon, once again, with the 187th Attack Helicopter Battalion flying 225 hours of combat in the War in Iraq. But the harsh conditions and human carnage had a devastating effect on Jesse, both physically and mentally, and he was discharged in December 2005 to the Ready Reserve. Nonetheless, it is amazing to think that in today's modern volunteer military, he would have still been reactivated at the bequest of the Pentagon, as he was approaching 70 years old.[3] Still, as so often demonstrated by the Marcel family, there was no need to ask him twice.

Through all the years since 1947, Jesse always supported his father's account of what actually crashed outside Roswell, New Mexico, in 1947. After all, when the boy Jesse arrived in the family kitchen after he was roused from his sleep on that warm July night, he saw what few others on this earth have ever experienced. It was a sight that remained vivid in his memory until the day he died, and we have always envied that fortuitous opportunity.

After appearing in 1980 on the popular ABC TV series *In Search Of,* hosted by Leonard Nimoy, Jesse called his son on return home to Houma, Louisiana. The former intelligence officer was excited that after 33 years he was able to return to the desert site where it had all started—where what should have begun the adventure of a lifetime became an embarrassment and blemish on the family reputation. With some trepidation, the elder Marcel walked the barren graze land describing the unusual debris he had gathered there back in 1947, and the TV show provided him with that rare opportunity to relive part of history. "It [the metal] was nothing made on this earth," was a statement he stood by until his death. He was already suffering from emphysema. Heavy smoking had taken its toll, his breathing became more labored, but still the thinner, dry air of the high desert provided some relief. Time was running out for the senior officer, and what was there to lose by finally speaking out? Now, with the passage of more than 30 years of broken promises from the government to someday reveal the truth, sadly, it was quite evident that the truth was not forthcoming. What could they do to a dying old man for finally stepping forward with the facts at the risk of drawing unwanted attention to a story they felt was buried back in 1947? As a doctor there was no hiding his condition, and his son preserved all the opportunities he still had with his fading father. Jesse tape-recorded the father-son phone conversation and what shined through just beyond the warmth and love for one another was the shared experience that skeptics have often tried to shake. But together, their resolve and conviction was one and the same. They would talk every week until the end, especially as his father opened up more and more publicly about Roswell.[4] That would all end on June 24, 1986.

It was early in 1990 that the Fund for UFO Research asked us to put together a selection of Roswell witnesses to participate in a special conference sponsored by Hans Adam II, the royal prince of Liechtenstein. Jesse was immediately notified and happily accepted.

Little did we realize that someone else would also start calling the doctor as well as one of the other invited military witnesses.

This was not the first time uninvited callers gave Roswell witnesses cause to remain silent. The public information officer (PIO) from the old Roswell Army Air Field, First Lieutenant Walter Haut, along with his wife, "Pete," described to us 30 years of threatening phone calls. "There were so many calls, I lost track of them," a disgusted Haut complained.[5] Long before caller ID, both he and his wife received menacing calls from the "Norseman," as he was dubbed, who repeatedly would shout into the phone "HOWT!" and next demand that 1947 "be forgotten." The other frequent caller actually identified himself as the "Shadow" and, on occasion, Walter's wife would pick up the phone from their bedside at 3 a.m. "Each and every time he called, he told me that my life was in jeopardy if I talked about the incident," complained Haut.

Sergeant Lloyd Thompson, of the RAAF's 393rd Bomb Squadron, was a B-29 crewman on the second "body" flight out of Roswell, which flew directly to Fort Worth Army Field Field in Fort Worth, Texas. Just as the Haut family had experienced many years of harassment, soon Thomson received a threatening phone call about attending the meeting in Washington. He had just moved to Alamogordo, New Mexico, and had an unlisted number, and the caller even addressed him by his old army nickname. After two such warnings, he quickly cancelled his trip.[6] The death threat was abundantly clear. The FBI was contacted and officially listed the complaint as a "death threat." No one was ever apprehended for this reported crime.

Next, Jesse and his wife Linda received calls that clearly suggested that he was being watched, and his family became more and more concerned about his safety. Still, Jesse was not about to be intimidated and continued to make plans for the trip out east—but not with his family. It wouldn't be safe.

One particular call did stand out. It, too, was anonymous, but it wasn't a warning. Rather, it was an invitation to meet with a high-ranking official while in Washington. It was an offer to help. Odd though, that the call was also prompted by an unpublicized, confidential meeting yet to take place. It sure raised a lot of attention for people meeting at the nation's capital to discuss something as silly as a "weather balloon" recovery at Roswell. Jesse's family became even more concerned about the trip—but a good soldier doesn't retreat. Jesse arrived in Washington, as did 11 other witnesses.[7]

Following the adjournment of this unprecedented meeting, Jesse followed the instructions from the unknown political official.[8] He took a cab, alone, to the Capitol Building. Each waiting second raised the specter of a setup. Even all of Jesse's military training left him with concern of a trap—40 years after the same U.S. government had covered up the truth about Roswell. Finally, a dark-suited man stepped out from a room and introduced himself as a staff member and senior senatorial counsel to Senator Robert C. Byrd. "Dr. Marcel, so pleased to meet you. My name is Dick D'Amato. Will you please follow me?" They would take an elevator to a deep underground conference room to talk in private. Jesse was still on his guard.

"Roswell is true, but then you already know that," stated the official. "The problem: It's buried deep within the black budget, and government funds have been spent since 1947 to keep the truth from coming out," explained D'Amato. "Whenever someone gets too close to the truth, they are immediately discredited. All of the main witnesses remain on their radar scopes," he warned Jesse.

"Have you or your family ever been threatened? Because I want to give you a private number to reach me directly if anyone ever does," offered D'Amato. They next returned to the ground level, and each wished the other good luck as they shook hands. For Jesse, a devout Catholic, the flight back to Montana provided a heightened sense of anxiety. "Dear God, please, just get me home."

Neither Jesse's father nor he had discussed the Roswell Incident publicly for almost 30 years. As Dr. Marcel observed, "doing so would pose a very real danger to our careers, if not our very lives." So when his dad finally broke his own silence in 1978 and spoke out as to the true nature of the UFO crash, Jesse, Jr., was also sought out by researchers—and by those responsible for the cover-up. But our position, as investigators, remained: The more light one shines on the situation, the more protection it provides. As long as our sources came out from the closet of secrecy, government reprisal was less likely. Still, phone calls and shadowy observers remained a persistent nuisance at the least. Jesse later commented, "While some members of our elected government, such as the official [D'Amato] with whom I met, know about the 'black government,' they discuss its existence very discreetly, if at all, knowing that all evidence of an extraterrestrial visitation can be made to disappear, and the elimination of an overly talkative government employee would be child's play." He added, "To this day I have kept that piece of paper [D'Amato's phone number] and have stored a copy of the info in a safe place, should the need for it ever arise."[9]

After the Washington conference, we became all the more committed to solving the mystery of what truly crashed outside of Roswell in 1947. Sworn affidavits were taken from a growing list of witnesses, and Congressman Steven Schiff of New Mexico was enlisted to represent constituents. With growing curiosity of specific events inspired by the crash of the unknown object back in 1947, we suggested the notion of hypnotic regression to Dr. Marcel, with the plan of taking him back to that night when he was awakened from his sleep and taken with his mother into the kitchen. Though hesitant, Jesse finally agreed, still arguing that he was a poor candidate, as he had never been hypnotized before. We next sought out one of the best in his field and secured Dr. John Watkins, professor emeritus in psychology from the University of Montana at

Missoula. Dr. Watkins was famous for getting one of the accused "Hillside Stranglers," Kenneth Bianchi, to confess under hypnosis. (During 60 hours of interviews and hypnosis, Bianchi also implicated his cousin, Angelo Buono.[10])

Next, to our pleasant surprise, NBC's *TODAY* show assigned a film crew to visually record the sessions with the full intent of later broadcast. Producers assured us that they considered Jesse, Jr., an unimpeachable witness with credentials that rivaled anyone they had interviewed before. They were just as fascinated as we were with the technique of hypnosis. In fact, it was one of the first times they had not requested filming a time-regression interview, the flying saucer story withstanding. Little did any of us know just how difficult an affair we were in for.

Call it professional resistance, doctor versus doctor; it took the better part of the day for Dr. Watkins to finally succeed placing Dr. Marcel in a hypnotic state. Ultimately, that evening, he was back in the early morning of July 8, 1947, describing the events as they unfolded in the Marcel kitchen. Jesse described how the metal-like debris was scattered over the floor with a sampling on the dining room table. He painted the picture of each of them handling the material and, in his trance, sketched the symbology that ran the lengths of I-beam members scattered within the other pieces. All the while we quietly passed handwritten questions to Dr. Watkins to ask Jesse, and the NBC film crew captured each moment. A most important element through the entire regression was that Jesse relived the entire situation in the first person. In other words, he was describing the entire scenario as though it was unfolding right before our eyes. And here's what was most critical: His father at no time mentioned that this was possibly any type of conventional device. Jesse recited over and over again how his dad called it a "flying saucer." The film crew stood dumbfounded.

Something we had not anticipated took place, though, as Jesse was brought out of his sleep regression. Mind you, his father had died in 1986, just four years before this project. When Jesse opened his eyes and took in his surroundings, he began to look from one side of the room to the other calling out, "Dad! Dad!" Tears began to stream down his face as it finally struck us: So intense, so real was the experience he had just relived with his father back in 1947, he felt that he had just lost him all over again. We were devastated and Jesse, aside from being physically exhausted, showed a pain in his face that we will never forget. What became of all the film footage shot by the NBC crew? Co-host Bryant Gumbel at *TODAY* decided that it was "too controversial" and opted not to "ever" show this most convincing hypnotic interview of Dr. Jesse Marcel. As one NBC reporter informed us, "It was too convincing."[11]

According to Jesse's wife, Linda, the unidentified callers persisted and always wanted to know where Jesse was. "Whenever Jess was scheduled for a 'Roswell' event, the calls would start. We began to wonder if our home was bugged."[12] Within the next few years, the U.S. government would demonstrate just how concerned they were with high-standing witnesses such as Jesse speaking out on the truth about Roswell.

In September 1994, the Pentagon called a press conference where Air Force Colonel Richard Weaver announced to the room full of reporters that they had a new theory to explain what had crashed in 1947. He explained that it was the same type of balloon comprised of Neoprene rubber, reflective foil, wooden sticks, string, and masking tape. But this time, it was part of a Top Secret project called Mogul, which in theory would monitor Soviet testing of atomic weapons.

The hieroglyphic-like symbols on the wreckage that Jesse and other witnesses described were merely flowers painted on Scotch tape. Major James McAndrew was the principal researcher of the special report and, for some reason, was especially annoyed that

Dr. Marcel would not back down from their new theory. After all, he was there in 1947; McAndrew wasn't even born. Jesse was about to receive new phone calls—from Major McAndrew. Each time he tried to persuade the ranking officer, Colonel Marcel, that what he actually saw and handled was nothing more than "masking tape, shrunk down into the shape of I-beams from the desert sun."[13] Each time, Jesse refused to accept such a "simplistic and ridiculous" explanation and politely stood by his personal account of the facts. McAndrew, becoming more and more frustrated, would yell into the phone, "What is it going to take for you to accept that all you saw was masking tape!" Jesse would never waver. After six futile attempts to force Jesse to retreat, McAndrew finally conceded, "Then I guess we'll never know what you actually saw back in 1947." Jesse had won—but not for long.

Skeptics such as the late Robert Todd and Karl Pflock targeted both Jesse's father and Jesse himself, and made efforts to smear their credibility—standard procedure within the U.S. government's "damage control" phase of containment. Young Jesse had to stand by and watch his father serve as the fall guy when the weather balloon explanation replaced what all involved knew to be the truth. Following his orders, the older Marcel had to convey to his son the same restrictions on the matter just placed on him. The occurrence was not to be discussed again, which made no sense to the boy after having been taught the importance of telling the truth—and the penalties for telling a lie. Making matters worse, his dad had to go along with it. After an official report is issued, should any dissention remain, it is to be ridiculed and discredited—immediately. Such has been "official" policy since the incident in 1947 and then has intensified since the Mogul report was presented, a form of "scorched witnesses" procedure. Todd, like Pflock, was one of the contributors to the newly prepared Air Force report. Through Freedom of Information (FOIA) requests, he managed to secure a copy of Jesse,

Sr.'s service files through the National Personnel Records Center. Displaying a total lack of knowledge of military record protocol, Todd used the tactic that if it wasn't in the file, it never happened. Exercising blatant deceit on his part, Todd, and other skeptics following his lead, attempted to destroy the reputation of Marcel solely on omissions of data. Ironically, when the late Congressman Steven Schiff commissioned the General Accounting Office (GAO) to conduct a document search for all records pertaining to the Roswell Incident of 1947, they discovered in 1995 that all the records from the RAAF (Roswell Army Air Field) at the time of the event were destroyed or at the very least missing. What's good for the goose is not good for the gander. According to Todd and Pflock, because Marcel's files from 1947 were missing, "he" was the liar. Still, his son Jesse stood firm in defending his father, but the War in Iraq had other plans.

Major Jesse Marcel, Sr., was the first military person at the crash site. Sworn to secrecy in 1947, he broke his silence 30 years later, thus igniting the civilian investigation of the Roswell Incident. Photo from July 8, 1947.

Upon his return from his first tour of active duty in Baghdad, Jesse was suffering from severe post-traumatic stress disorder (PTSD). The slightest loud noise caused him to jump from his chair or dive to the floor. This is often experienced by military combatants exposed to the loud noise of explosives. The nightmares and flashbacks of dead Iraqi babies were devastating to him. War poet Wilfred Owen once wrote, "Men whose minds the dead have ravished." Still, he made a second tour, which sadly ruined his physical health. Before, Jesse was an avid biker, skier, and motorcycle rider. He ran and kept himself in tip-top physical shape. He came home from the war wearing leg braces. The deployment would cost him his medical practice. He lost the control of his hands, and for a surgeon this forced his retirement. The army had seen fit to recall Jesse because he was a medical doctor. His days of healing the sick were left behind in the war, and in return, the army refused to promote him for his service.[14]

After Iraq, Jesse remarked that he finally understood his father's disillusionment and bitterness with the military following Roswell. His dad was ordered to be the "fall guy" in 1947 with the promise that the truth would all come out within a few years, and his son Jesse remained a "good soldier" by keeping such feelings private. Jesse knew the truth about Roswell, and no government or military could tell him otherwise.[15]

In May 2013, Jesse was once again called back to Washington, DC, to testify with us as part of the Roswell panel at the Citizen's Hearing on UFOs. For five full days, UFO researchers and witnesses from all over the world presented their best evidence to a panel of six former U.S. congresspeople. Jesse was one of the most moving of the participants and also offered a closing statement on behalf of all the deceased Roswell witnesses. No doubt, his father would have been very proud. Even in his frail and failing condition, his son was still in the fight; the old Jesse was back, but it would be his last battle.

Within days after the hearings, his daughter Denise would inform us that her dad felt the need to go back to Roswell—one last time. Arrangements were quickly made for one of our last surviving witnesses to the granddaddy of all UFO cases to be the guest of honor at the 2013 annual Roswell UFO Festival. One last time, he went out to the debris site where his father had gathered all the unusual wreckage back in 1947. One last time, he went back to his childhood home and stood in the kitchen where it all began for him.

It was as though it all had happened yesterday. Dr. Jesse Marcel had come full circle and now was content—at peace. No one was ever able to rob him of what he knew to be the truth. No government was able to take that away from him.

Don Schmitt (left) with Jesse Marcel, Jr. (front center) and the family of Joe Brazel (Mack's grandson) at the UFO Museum in Roswell, New Mexico. Photo from 2009.

Jesse's apprehensions were entirely correct. A little more than a month later, he quietly passed away at his home while reading a book—about UFOs.[16] Try as they might, Roswell was forever etched into his very soul—a soul now reunited with his parents. The father, and a son, who handled pieces of a craft from another planet and were courageous enough to take those of us who would listen along for the journey. The valiant soldier had won his war. A star is shining brighter over New Mexico, and so we gaze up and smile. The truth is eternal and, thanks to Dr. Jesse Marcel, so is Roswell.

CHAPTER 7

Nightmare in the Emergency Room

From all eyewitness accounts, something suspicious was happening inside the Roswell Army Air Field (RAAF) hospital at the time of all the rumors about the crash of a flying saucer just north of town. Outside doctors and nurses rushed throughout the halls and into and out of rooms that had been designated off-limits to the regular staff. The normally assigned staff were relieved of their duties and sent back to their quarters until further notified. The variety wings of the complex, despite all of the commotion, were eerily quiet except for guarded whispers. Nothing was to be openly discussed without permission, as though those allowed to stay remained on auto-pilot to complete their clandestine work. MPs were positioned around the outside perimeter as well posted inside the main emergency corridor. Ambulance trucks would hurriedly pull up to the rear loading dock, which led directly to the emergency room. As First Lieutenant Rosemary A. McManus, a regular nurse assigned to the RAAF medical unit, described to us just weeks before passing away in Eau Claire, Wisconsin, in 1994, "Something big had happened."[1] She declined to acknowledge anything more.

Lieutenant Colonel Harold M. Warne was a highly experienced hospital administrator who, as a doctor, had been exposed to the worst human atrocities during WWII. Even in 1947, planes would occasionally crash during training exercises, and bodies mangled and burned beyond repair had become all too common at the world's first atomic base. But nothing in Warne's medical schooling prepared him for this. Something big had happened, and it was not part of any medical journal. And what became especially insulting was that even though Warne was in charge of the RAAF medical unit, he was not cleared for this situation—a situation he personally knew not to be based on mere rumor. Therein may be the cause of his behavior as opportunities would later present themselves.

RAAF base hospital, where the alien bodies were taken for cursory examination prior to being flown out. Photo circa 1947.

All military hospital administrators had their own executive secretary. Dr. Warne's was a 27-year-old civilian woman named Miriam "Andrea" Bush. Bush was a graduate of New Mexico State College at Las Cruces, where she majored in Business Administration. During WII, college campuses were principal recruiting centers for the FBI, and young women like Bush saw the allure of such a lifestyle. That lifestyle required one to be unmarried, in no relationship, and free to be assigned most anywhere in the country. According to Bush's family, she specialized in intelligence, which would explain why she was hired by the military for a Top Secret job at the RAAF after the surrender of Japan.[2]

Now, one item of crucial importance needs to be emphasized here: The RAAF hospital in 1947 did not have a morgue. That is precisely why the base had a contract with a private mortuary: the Ballard Funeral Home. The city of Roswell did not have its own coroner at that time, so it relied on Chaves County to provide such assistance. All reports of extra security and the presence of outside medical personnel took place at the exact same time of the purported crash of the flying saucer outside of town. If civilian fatalities were involved, they would have been sent directly to one of Roswell's two funeral homes. The other was LaGrone, and both it and Ballard are still in business today.[3] If there were military fatalities, they would have gone first to the base hospital and then to the private mortuary. Curious phone inquiries were made to the Ballard Funeral Home regarding the availability of children's caskets. This was a rather bizarre request on the face of it, but even more so coming from a facility without a morgue—and, more importantly, no children were ever reported to have died from any cause on the base during the entire month of July 1947. Why the need for child-size caskets? Dry ice was called in from Clardy's Dairy in Roswell during this same period of time. Subsequently, there were follow-up calls to the mortician asking questions about recommended embalming techniques that would be the least detrimental to biological tissue and bodily fluids. Something big had happened, and it appeared that the RAAF hospital had in its possession a number of bodies beyond the realm of standard and regulated state law. In any event, the absence of a morgue notwithstanding, the base hospital would have to temporarily serve for whatever "bodies" superseded legal protocol.[4]

Glenn Dennis was a Roswell embalmer in 1947 who claimed to have had a run-in with military authorities at the RAAF base hospital after receiving phone calls from the base requesting child-sized caskets. Photo from 2000.

It was dinnertime one evening during one of the days highlighted by all of those strange circumstances when Miriam Bush arrived at her parent's home from a rather unsettling day at the base hospital. She sat down to eat in the dining room with her mother and father, who was the first chiropractor to set up a practice in Roswell; her brother, George; and her sister, Jenny. Many years later, both George and Jenny recounted how upset their sister became as she pushed her food aside.

She became panic-stricken as she started to weep uncontrollably and raced toward her bedroom. The entire family had great respect for her employment at the base. Did she lose her job? A close friend? George sensed something worse—more sinister. "Fear seemed to overcome her," he said.[5] Dr. Bush reacted immediately and he went to her aide.

He found his daughter lying on her bed as she continued sobbing. Finally, her father was able to calm her enough to learn what was distressing her so terribly. The story she would confide was told between tears and near-shock. It all would sound like a bad dream, but her emotional behavior was all too real. It was something she was never prepared for. None of them were. This nightmare was for real. Slowly, she was able to verbalize exactly what the cause of it was.

She had been performing all of her regular duties at the hospital earlier that day, but grew more and more curious about all of the additional personnel who seemed to be relieving the regular staff. So when her boss, Dr. Warne, took her by the arm and led her aside, she expected either an explanation or that she, too, would be dismissed for the day. Instead, whether out of frustration from being left out of all the commotion or merely just the human desire to share all of the excitement with one of the few local staff on hand, Warne cautiously walked her to the examination room. Upon entering, surroundings that otherwise would have been quite familiar to Bush demonstrated something she did not anticipate. She was immediately taken aback to observe a number of bodies on gurneys in the middle of the room. But something was wrong. Something was terribly wrong. At first she quietly cried out, "My God! They're children!" But she soon realized that their body size was the only child-like quality. Their skin was grayish to brown in tone, and white linens covered most of each figure. But the heads—the heads were too large. And those eyes, those large eyes that wouldn't shut. "Those staring eyes," she cried. Panic started to quicken her heart rate, and then it happened: "One of them moved!"[6] All her father could do was hold her and listen in total disbelief as she wept. He was aware of all the talk in town about the crashed spaceship outside of town and the crew of little men. But now it had touched his own family, and there was little if anything he could do to remedy the pain in his daughter's mind. Eventually she would cry herself to sleep, though one might argue whether sleep would serve as any respite. Mental exhaustion was more likely the reason.

Mornings can be a blessing or a resumption of the same pain experienced the night before. Miriam's professional training tried to engage and, with little thought, her fear grew more and more into anger at her boss. "Why did he have to show me something so upsetting?" became her primary motivator for returning to confront

Dr. Warne. But just as important, the entire town of Roswell was abuzz with all the talk about the crashed flying saucer and the small men who piloted it. Only the base south of town could provide the answers, and only the hospital knew the whole truth. The morning newspaper carried headlines about all the excitement being over some old weather balloon. How silly, she thought.[7]

Much had taken place overnight while Miriam played the same scenario in her mind over and over again. Maybe she imagined that the next time all that disturbed her would somehow magically change. Base personnel, who had forgone sleep, dealt with the reality that commanded their full attention: A temporary morgue was hastily set up, a full-scale recovery operation was taking place at another site further to the northwest of town, and another body site was located. Most all of the clandestine activity at the hospital was on hold at least for the time being—as though nothing big had ever happened. The day was Wednesday, July 9th, and Miriam's fate for the rest of her life was about to be sealed.

As did so many others who were merely performing their duties at the RAAF, Miriam immediately became suspect. Any base personnel and employees who saw anything out of the ordinary had to be warned of the consequences of speaking out of turn, and the traumatized secretary was no exception. Her brother, George, somberly described to us her demeanor that evening, as she said, "I am never to say another word about what I saw. None of you ever heard me say anything about it,"[8] she chided them. According to her brother and her sister, Jenny, she displayed all the symptoms of being subjected to heavy-handed threats. She would become more and more paranoid about the entire ordeal. Yet she couldn't share even her worst fears with the very family who also knew the truth. There was nothing any of them could do and certainly nothing any of them could prove. The entire situation became rather hopeless. Best to do just as the military sternly advised—never to say another word, as though it never happened. In many ways Miriam could then try to convince herself that it was nothing more than a nightmare. Unfortunately for her, the images of what she witnessed in that examination room were etched in her very psyche, and those who observed her realized she wouldn't let it go. She would need to be watched.

No one ever questioned Miriam's truthfulness, and she refused to ever discuss the incident again. Her fear and paranoia were two-sided: both the haunting images of what she experienced *and* the concern for government reprisal. But it had also made a lasting impression on her brother. When George married Patricia, it was one of the very first private pieces of family history he confided to her.[9] Sadly, no one in Miriam's immediate family was able to penetrate the wall of silence built around her. Whatever she saw in that hospital examination room in 1947 tormented her relentlessly. She would marry within a year—someone she had just met—move to California, and try to forget the unforgettable.[10]

After nearly 40 years of a loveless, childless, "arranged" marriage, she would finally file for divorce in 1987. A tremendous weight was lifted off her shoulders; she was not distraught or depressed about the failed relationship. Ironic that she was casting aside part of her past—which all began in a Roswell hospital room back in 1947. Such was the distinct impression from her sister-in-law, Pat, who spoke to her over the phone on a regular basis. Within months of the marriage breakup, Pat sensed a subtle change becoming the focus of each new conversation: Miriam was becoming increasingly paranoid, according to Pat. She was deeply concerned about being watched and followed, which, to Miriam's sister, Jenny, all seemed to be connected in some way to 1947 and the objective of a 40-year marriage to a gay man.[11] It appeared that shadowy figures had taken his place, albeit from a distance.

During December 1989, Patricia Bush would receive another phone call from Miriam, but it would be the last time anyone would hear from her. She had become obsessed with the fear that someone was spying on her day-to-day activities. Nothing Pat could tell her would alleviate her dread. Still, no one in the family suspected that time was about to run out for Miriam.

The very next day, Miriam registered into a motel just north of San Jose, California, in the small town of Fremont. If she had no intention of drawing any attention to the family, she mistakenly checked in using her sister Jenny's name. She was unaccompanied, and no one saw her again until the next morning. The coroner's report concluded that she had taken her own life by wrapping a plastic bag around her head, a rather prolonged and gruesome way to commit suicide. In fact, statistically it is seldom done in that manner. What was not publicized was that there were fresh scratches and bruises all over her arms. Other suspicious details, such as no prearrangements with her insurance providers or a suicide note, were not considered by investigators.[12] Jenny believed that her sister was sending a message by the use of her name. "Something was not right, and it was her way of letting us know," she remarked.[13] Miriam's own suspicions and fears may not have been totally unfounded. The truth she possessed about Roswell died with her—death being the ultimate silencer.

Within a few years of Miriam's death, investigator Victor Golubic tracked down Dr. Jack Comstock, who had served as the RAAF chief surgeon in 1947. Not only didn't Dr. Comstock have any memory of the unearthly patients, but he also had no memory of former hospital associate Miriam Bush[14]—denial being the second greatest silencer.

CHAPTER 8

Richards's Cave

I know where it's at. He used to keep stuff in there that he didn't want others to find.

—L.D. Sparks

*T*he search for physical evidence from the Roswell UFO crash of 1947 has been one of the most frustrating aspects of our quarter-century investigation of this case. We learned early on from interviewing those RAAF (Roswell Army Air Field) airmen who were part of the cleanup operations at the three crash locations that some of them might have pocketed pieces of the strange wreckage. In fact, all those who came in contact with the wreckage—whether during the week-long cleanup out in the desert, or transporting the wreckage back to the RAAF base near Roswell, or guarding the wreckage in the big hangar at the base, or crating-up the wreckage for shipment out of the base—all had the opportunity to sneak a piece of the exotic "metal" for themselves. How many of them tried and were successful, we will never know, but we are convinced that some of them were, and somehow were able to secret their purloined "prizes" past the probing eyes of their ever-present overseers.

One of these was Captain Oliver "Pappy" Henderson, a pilot with the First Air Transport Unit at the RAAF in 1947, who flew the first load of wreckage out from the base to Wright Field in Dayton, Ohio. Years later, after Henderson had passed away, we learned from a longtime friend of his, John Kromschroeder, a dentist with an avid interest in metallurgy, that Henderson had kept a piece of the wreckage.[1] In 1979, according to Kromschroeder, Henderson showed him a small piece of metal that Henderson said had come from the 1947 crash. Very thin but very strong, it resembled gray aluminum. Henderson told him that it was a piece of some of the lighter metal that lined the interior of the craft. According to Henderson, when the material was energized, it produced "perfect illumination"—a soft light with no shadows.[2] Unfortunately for us, after Henderson's passing in 1986, his strange piece of metal could not be found. Kromschroeder thought that at some point "Pappy" simply sent it back to the Air Force.[3]

Other military personnel were also said to have kept pieces of the UFO wreckage for themselves. Major Jesse Marcel, the first military person to the crash site on the Brazel/Foster ranch, was said to have buried a piece of the so-called "memory metal" under a concrete patio in the back of his house on W. 7th Street in Roswell, or maybe it was placed in a seam somewhere in the extensive stone wall that encased the backyard of his house. We checked the stone wall without any luck, but the concrete patio now forms the base floor of one of the rooms now inside of the house, and none of the owners of the house since we have been on the case have been sympathetic to our requests to play "Geraldo Rivera Meets Al Capone's Safe" with one of their interior floors.

Right across the street from the old Marcel house stands the old residence of the former public information officer (PIO) at the RAAF base in 1947, Walter Haut. We knew Walter as a friend for many years until his passing in 2005. We suspected, but he did not confirm it until the release of his sealed statement after his death, the extent of his true involvement in the 1947 UFO crash-retrieval.[4] Haut had indeed visited one of the crash sites and was later seen showing a piece of the wreckage that he had in his possession to some of his cohorts on the base, as had been told to us a few years earlier by one of his subordinates.[5] Following up on that earlier lead, we located someone in Roswell who told us that the father of a former work associate of his was a former RAAF civilian employee who was living in a nursing home somewhere in Texas. He told his son that back in 1947 that some of the RAAF base officers had received "tokens" of the UFO incident and that Walter Haut was one of those officers. According to the story, Haut kept his "token" in the crawl space of his house on W. 7th Street. According to his daughter Julie, the original house did not have a crawl space, but the family-room addition, built in the early 1950s, did.[6] She described to us how, on one occasion, she walked into the family room, surprising "Padre" (the appellation she always used to refer to her father) as he was quickly placing something back between a loose fieldstone in the fireplace. She said that she always suspected that location but also felt that the crawl space under the family room was a possibility.[7] By the time we got this information, however, Walter had already moved into a nursing home, which is why, according to co-author Don Schmitt, he and Julie spent so much time going through Walter's personal effects—unsuccessfully, as it turned out—looking for that "token" of the 1947 incident. Now, Julie, another child of Roswell, is gone.

Robert Scroggins was a New Mexico state police officer in the summer of 1947. He had an office northwest of Roswell in Corona and lived in Hobbs, southeast of Roswell. We know that Mack Brazel had gone into Corona from the J.B. Foster Ranch he managed seeking answers as to what had crashed on his ranchland and who he should contact about it. He took some pieces of wreckage, with him, which he passed around to, among others, fellow patrons of "Wade's Bar" to examine and offer their opinions.[8] At some point while in Corona, Brazel met up with Scroggins, who told Brazel that he was heading home to Hobbs but would be happy to stop off in Roswell with a piece of the wreckage to show officials there to see what he could find out. We know that he stopped at the Roswell City Fire Station and passed the piece of "memory metal" around to those present (including 12-year-old Frankie Dwyer, who was there waiting for her fireman father; see Chapter 4) to everyone's utter amazement.[9] Word of Scroggins's visit apparently traveled at "warp-speed" to the city administration officials, as Roswell's city manager, C.M. Woodbury, soon thereafter paid a visit to the firehouse admonishing them not to go to the crash site just north of town. Woodbury no doubt also notified his "good friend" Colonel William Blanchard, the RAAF base commander, of Scroggins's visit, as soon thereafter the Roswell firehouse was paid another surprise visit—this time by a "colonel from the base" warning the firemen to stay away from the crash site.[10] By the time Scroggins reached his home in Hobbs, he had been relieved of the "memory metal" Brazel had given him. We later interviewed as many of Scroggins's alleged six wives as we could find, and none of them recalled ever seeing the strange piece of metal.

In 2005, we interviewed the son of a former Roswell City Police officer, Eugene Smith, who had apparently gotten to one of the crash sites in some unknown capacity. Smith, Jr., recalled his father coming home one evening at the time of the crashed flying saucer business in 1947 holding a rectangular piece of metal. It was fairly regular in shape, about 3 or 4 inches wide by 6 to 10 inches long by about 1 inch thick. It looked like aluminum, but it was very heavy for its size—so heavy, in fact, that they used it as a doorstop at their house for many years. "When I asked my father where he had gotten it, he just said, 'From a flying saucer that crashed north of here.'"[11] His father had passed away some years before, so we couldn't question him about his find. That being the case, we of course wanted to know if the "doorstop" was still in his son's possession. But, like all of the other such cases of an alleged piece of the wreckage being in someone's family for years, this one, too, had disappeared into the ether and became lost to father time over the passage of years. Smith, Jr., recalled, "No. I no longer have it. It must have gotten lost when we moved and we threw a lot of stuff out. I don't know."[12]

Likewise, Thomas Gonzales had been a sergeant in the RAAF motor pool in July 1947. We tracked him down to Houston, Texas, and interviewed him in person in 2000. He said that he had been called out to help with the cleanup at one of the crash sites, and in the process he pocketed a few small pieces of the wreckage for himself. He told us that he had kept these pieces "on top of the TV set" for years, but that in the course of several moves over the years, he had no idea where they were or what became of them.[13] Where had we heard one that before? It appears that one of the salient properties of the crash wreckage is its propensity for disappearing over time!

We are now satisfied that the explosion of the Roswell UFO occurred 75 miles northwest of Roswell late in the evening of July 2, 1947, near the town of Corona. We also know that the rancher William W. "Mack" Brazel discovered the crash wreckage in a sheep pasture on his ranch, which was owned by J.B. Foster, who lived in Texas, the following morning of July 3, 1947. With Brazel was a young boy from a neighboring ranch, 7-year-old Timothy "Dee" Proctor. (See Chapter 1.) We also know that the military did not arrive in force at the ranch to commence the cleanup of the crash site until late the following Tuesday, the 8th of July. Even though the high desert region around Corona did not receive full telephone service until 1986, word of unusual things happening, like airplane crashes out in the nearby desert area, traveled quickly to the surrounding ranches. It was almost like a "family affair" for the ranch owners, their children, and the ranch hands and their children to visit such crash sites to see what had happened, to help anyone who might need help, and to retrieve "souvenirs." And it was no different in the case of a crashed spaceship from another world.

The ranch population in the Corona area and to some extent the ranchers just northwest of Roswell had about five days all to themselves to pick over the wreckage before the military arrived and secured the crash sites. It stands to reason that any number of "souvenirs" must have been successfully retrieved by the adults *and children* before the military got there. Little bodies with big heads and funny eyes were also seen, which required an especially harsh response by the military, one that seems to have affected the children at least as much as the adults.

Dee Proctor is discussed in depth elsewhere in this book. Suffice it to say here, because he refused to ever be interviewed at length about what he witnessed in Brazel's sheep pasture or what might have happened to him afterward at the hands of the military, most of what we know about him was obtained from his mother, the late Loretta Proctor, who, with her husband, Floyd, were Mack Brazel's nearest neighbors.[14] Something had terrified him into a stony silence that nobody, not even members of his own family, could break through to get him to talk about what happened out there in the desert. We, as investigators, tried on several occasions to ambush interview him, but he always somehow was able to avoid us. The closest we ever got was one day, as we were entering the front door of his mother's house to interview her and hopefully Dee, we heard the back door quickly slam shut. Dee had escaped again!

Years later, Dee would partially break a near-50-year silence when he packed his sick mother (he thought she might be near death) into his pickup truck for a bumpy ride out into the desert to a location at the base of a bluff some 2 1/2 miles east of the Brazel "debris field site." He stopped his truck, pointed upward toward the ridge atop the bluff, and said, "Here is where Mack found *something else.*"[15] That's all he said. His mother couldn't get him to say any more than that—ever. Dee Proctor died in 2006, a morbidly obese alcoholic. The ridge atop the bluff where he took his sick mother that day is now known as the "Dee Proctor Body Site," where we believe several occupants of the alien craft met their fate after being blown out when the ship exploded.[16]

Roswell photographer Jack Rodden did business with many of the ranchers from the Corona area. We had the opportunity to interview Rodden on a number of occasions many years after the 1947 event. He told us of one Corona rancher who said that his three kids had come home one day at the time of the incident frightened to death but refusing to talk about what they had seen. Rodden pressed the rancher, and the old-timer stated that his kids had gotten too close to *something*, and someone in the military (Lieutenant Arthur Philbin or Colonel Hunter Penn?) had scared them badly.[17]

Other area parents emotionally recounted how their children were never the same after encountering somebody or *something*: "When they returned home, they looked as though they had seen a ghost!" Others remarked, "They [the kids] were frightened, shocked, and grew increasingly paranoid."[18] Was it just seeing small pieces of wreckage that had scared them, or had they been to the second location 2 1/2 miles east of the debris field? And, having been caught doing so, was the military forced to take them aside to "put the fear of God" into them to never talk about what they had seen? Most of these youngsters, grown adults today, have still refused to talk about it, even with their families.[19] One who did talk, however, was the son of a former ranch hand on a ranch close to the debris field site as well as the body site. Sydney "Jack" Wright lamented how he "grew up overnight" from the images of what he witnessed out in the desert atop a ridge as a child, images that still haunt him to this day: "There were bodies, small bodies with big heads and eyes.... We couldn't get away from there fast enough."[20] For some kids, not quite fast enough, Jack. Not quite fast enough.

We first heard about Dan Richards from Mack Brazel's son, Bill. In an early interview with him, Bill told us that, among the Corona ranchers, we should especially check out the Richards family. Their ranch was located past Hines Draw, not far (5–8 miles) from the Brazel/Foster Ranch debris field where most of the crash wreckage had been recovered. He also recalled that the Richards' son Dan was known to have been a "pack-rat," someone who "collected" (i.e., illegally obtained) lots of things. "He was one of those boys who was always where he shouldn't be," according to Bill.[21]

There are lots caves and sinkholes in the Corona area. Nothing mysterious, idiosyncratic, or nefarious about that. Millions of years ago, the entire western part of North America east of the Rocky Mountain Chain was covered by a vast but shallow Inland Sea. Over the course of countless thousands of millennia, the skeletal remains of tiny marine organisms such as corals and foraminifera were deposited on the seabed floor, with the resulting buildup of calcium carbonite forming sedimentary rock beds of what we know today as limestone. Limestone happens to be soluble in water, which, geologically speaking, has led to the formation of all of the cave systems and sinkholes we see in the world today, due to erosion of lime bed strata from their interaction with naturally occurring water.

The rumor was that Dan Richards had stored all of his contraband, which may have included U.S. Army ordnance, in one of the many of the caves and open caverns surrounding the Richards' ranch. "It was more of a pit than a cave," according to Bill Brazel, suggesting that he had actually seen it.[22] Bill then described for us a large, underground sinkhole—not a cave—the opening to the outside of which was at the top (the roof) rather than on the side, as a cave's would be:

A metal spike was driven into the rock at the cave-entrance to hold a rope, because it was a 60-ft. drop from the entrance to the floor of the cave. Once inside, the main chamber was so large that it was called "The Stadium." I went down in there one time many years ago. The light wasn't good, and I didn't stay there very long. All I could see were some empty cigar boxes strewn about the floor.[23]

Don Schmitt kneeling atop the entrance to Richards's cave, which is actually an underground sinkhole that has collapsed upon itself. Photo from 2000.

Bill concluded his Dan Richards retrospective by giving us the bad news that Richards was dead, having been killed in a solo auto accident in 1950. The youngster had just gotten his driver's license when he lost control of his pickup and it hit a telephone pole.[24]

Almost a full decade would go by before we revisited the case of Dan Richards again. We were interviewing a Roswell gentleman by the name of L.D. Sparks. We knew that Sparks had been with Mack Brazel's neighbor Floyd Proctor back in 1947 when they had witnessed Brazel on a Roswell sidewalk in the "escort" of a number of military personnel. We wanted to learn from Sparks all that he could remember regarding that brief encounter on that day so long ago. At some point in the interview, Sparks mentioned the name of Dan Richards and said that he knew him when they were both young teenagers.

Sparks had more details than Bill Brazel had about the nature of what Richards had stored in his secret cave. He described for

us his handling of what we now refer to as "memory metal" from the 1947 crash wreckage. He said that Richards had somehow "retrieved" an Army rifle and used the piece of "memory metal" for target practice. Sparks described how Dan Richards had him toss a thin piece of the foil-like material into the air as Richards fired his Army rifle at it. "Shot after shot just ricocheted off it," Sparks claimed. "I would crumble the piece into a ball and watch in amazement as it would unfold as it floated softly through the air."[25] Sparks also added that, like what happened to Bill Brazel's cigar box full-of-crash-debris in 1949, the military showed up at the Richards ranch to check out Dan about the same time. (Remember the empty cigar boxes Bill Brazel saw in Dan's cave.) Also like Bill Brazel, Sparks said that the "cave" was more of a sinkhole than a cave, and that, since the time of the incident, it had

Roswell rancher L.D. Sparks told of throwing pieces of "memory metal" into the air for Dan Richards to shoot at with a rifle as they floated to the ground and also provided the authors with directions to Dan Richards's "cave." Photo from 2000.

become "unsafe." He also knew where it was located but, at his advanced age, he could not take us there.[26]

Our investigation visited the Richards ranch in 2005 to find out what we could find out about Dan Richards' "cave." The dusty ranch itself was a cross somewhere between *Green Acres* and *Jurassic Park,* except that T-rex fortunately did not make an appearance. It was run by a woman named Suzy Manes who said she was the niece or cousin of the long-deceased Dan Richards. We had interviewed her over the telephone prior to our trip to the ranch. She indicated that she might have some information for us, not only about Dan's cave, but she thought that her mother had kept a diary for the year 1947! She didn't know where it was at that moment, but she was sure that she could find it by the time we arrived.

As we entered the Richards ranch house, we were overcome by the reek of stale cigarette smoke (neither of the authors has ever smoked). Through this foggy haze of smoke and fumes, we found the dining room table and sat down. "You boys want a smoke?" our hostess offered. As we struggled with that question, in walked a short, gruffy fellow looking for all the world like one of the "banditos" from the 1960 movie. He sat down at the table opposite Carey and, glowering, barked at him, "You a lawyer? If you are, I'll come over there and kill ya!" Then, turning to Schmitt, who was dressed in his desert garb of all black outerwear including black Gucci wingtips, he said, "And you look like a revenuer to me. The same goes for you!"[27]

Through burning eyes, we were able to assure our would-be executioner that we were not who he thought we were. It took some doing; maybe it was the horrified looks on our faces, but we got Trini Chavez to back off. After that, he turned out to be a friendly sort, and he had a very interesting story of his own to tell.

One of the young sons of a hired hand from the Richards ranch back in 1947, along with a couple of other boys, surreptitiously observed the military cleanup operation going on at the Foster ranch crash site from a distant hill. His name was Trinidad "Trini" Chavez. He recalled, "There were soldiers lined up and picking up all this material. Trucks and jeeps surrounded the area. We saw men with rifles get out of one of the trucks. Well, we figured we saw enough."[28] Unknown to Trini at the time, young Dan Richards had already "retrieved" a few of the "memory metal" pieces of wreckage, as had Trini's own father as well. But it was too late for Trini to take a piece for himself. "Too many damn soldiers," Trini lamented.[29] As for Trini's father, who was a hired hand on the Richards' ranch, he hid his piece of wreckage under a floor board in one of the sheds on the ranch. But one day the military came out, tore up the wooden floor boards of the shed, and found the piece. Both Trini and his father were warned, as were young Dan Richards and his parents, to remain silent—*or else!*[30] Did the military find Dan Richards's cave? We will never know for sure, of course, but the empty cigar boxes seen by Bill Brazel therein sometime after the incident suggest that they may have.

After first threatening the authors, Trinidad "Trini" Chavez told them that he and Dan Richards had witnessed the military cleaning up the "Debris Field [Crash] Site" on the Foster ranch and that his father had retrieved a piece of the wreckage, which he placed in a shed. Photo from 2005.

Suzy Manes still hadn't found her mother's 1947 diary when we asked her about it that day. (She *still* hasn't, which leads us to conclude that there never was one, but it was interesting while the thought lasted.) She also didn't know where Dan's cave was. She thought it was close to the ranch house and may have even opened into one of the house bedrooms! We looked. It didn't. As we were getting ready to leave, we noticed that Suzy was cooking something on the stove. In a large pot was what appeared to be the entire hind-quarter—hair and all—of a small animal. While Carey was looking on in horror for the nearest exit, Schmitt's stomach was making strange noises, Suzy then interjected, "It's lamb chops. Can you boys stay for dinner?" With that, we bid adieu, faster than a speeding bullet.

Yes, based upon the various descriptions and directions we had received over the years, our investigation finally did locate and visit what we believe was Dan Richards's "cave." It was a sinkhole that had collapsed upon itself. The original opening with the metal spike embedded was still there to be seen. Since the collapse, however, the "cave" had been fenced off by authorities as a danger to visitors like us and especially to spelunkers looking to do what they do best. So, we do not plan on trying to enter the "cave" anytime soon, as the rest of the roof of "The Stadium" sinkhole could collapse at any time—or not—but the risk is too great to take a chance.

Unfortunately, we'll never know for sure what became of Dan Richards's potential proof of alien visitation. Richards himself was killed just a few years after the 1947 incident in a single-vehicle accident. And, true, it is very conceivable that the long chain of caves and sinkholes that still surround his parents' ranch may have been too large a haystack, even for the military to tackle—as it remains for present-day researchers. Deep in the bowels of the old Richards' ranch, however, buried treasure may still lurk, yet to be discovered.

CHAPTER 9

The Little Houdini Who Made a Flying Saucer Disappear

*I*f one were to examine a plot of the former Roswell Army Air Field (RAAF) in 1947, you would note that the one entrance to the base that provided the utmost security from observation was the east gate. Since we began our investigation in 1989, we have had numerous civilian witnesses describe the convoy transporting the remains of the crashed ship detour from down town Roswell on Main Street, to the east side of town, and continue south to then enter unobserved through that specific side entrance. And what should be directly across the tarmac upon entering through that gate? Hangar P-3, which today is known as Building 84. From all accounts, this is precisely where all the material and remains from the multiple crash sites were deposited before being shipped to other secure locations—most notably Wright Field in Dayton, Ohio. As a matter of fact, there was an entire row of hangars and aircraft service buildings along that east end of the base that served as a total wall to provide total privacy from the rest of the base. It is no wonder that this served as the perfect hiding place until the retrieval operation was complete, and the final shipping destinations were determined. Additionally, we have secured the testimony of many of the personnel assigned to those same facilities who described that they were ordered not to report for their normal work detail and stay away from the area for a couple of days. Not that they didn't all suspect what was going down as to the nature of the quarantine. More importantly, the chances of their accidentally seeing something they shouldn't would be eliminated. All in all, the increased security measures worked.

Running parallel to the east fence line just 100 feet outside ran the old Southwest Pacific rail lines. The tracks merged with rail systems that spidered throughout the country.

Unlike many military bases that were established over operating train tracks, which enabled them to regularly use the freight lines for shipping purposes, the RAAF was a top security base and could not allow such a possible breach of security. It had to rely on a train line just outside of "the wall," so to speak.

To facilitate the base's use of the train, a freight yard was set up to accommodate special loading and unloading operations. As the first Strategic Air Command base in the world, the RAAF conducted such situations within standard security measures. MPs would often accompany the transporting of certain shipments until they reached their final destinations. So it came to us as no surprise that numerous witnesses to the events surrounding the incident of 1947 have mentioned the use of the railroad to ship some of the evidence out of town.

As it often has been demonstrated how many roads from Roswell led to the state of Ohio, the following account, if not for numerous stories involving the Roswell freight yard, would remain just another anecdote. We'll let you decide.

Ralph A. Multer received a Purple Heart medal after serving in the Navy during WWII. After leaving the service, he became a truck driver at the Timken Company of Canton, Ohio. Timken was heavily contracted during the war, providing ball bearings and steel tubing for military applications. Timken also was one of the largest wartime producers of large gun barrels. The company possessed major security clearances with the Pentagon. It also had a metallurgical furnace, a blast furnace that was one of the hottest in the world—more than 2,000 degrees Fahrenheit.[1]

On a number of occasions, we have heard how some of the GIs at the 1947 Roswell Army Air Field sneaked some small samples of wreckage from the crash to a garage just outside the base. There, they had an auto mechanic try to deform a piece with a welding arc. Just as with every other described attempt, even an acetylene torch couldn't affect the metallurgical characteristic of the strange material.[2] If such accounts are true, and based on all the testimony that paint visions of nothing but failed attempts at cracking the fracture point of "the stuff," it is reasonable to assume that they would have tried extreme heat. Timken would have provided a facility to conduct such a test. Unlike the steel-making center of Pittsburgh, Timken made its own steel to insure supply and quality control. And just as important, it was heavily contracted by the U.S. government, and it was just down the road, so to speak, from Wright Field. Something had to break the material's molecular code, and Timken could blast it in its furnace.

Multer, who had a security clearance with Timken, apologized to his wife, Violet. Instead of meeting her for lunch upon completing his shift, as he routinely did, he was sent out to the railroad yard with his truck. A special cargo had arrived from New Mexico and it needed to be hauled over to the Timken plant. Something covered by a canvas tarpaulin was loaded into his truck. FBI officials oversaw the procedure, which only added to the mystery of the assignment. Whatever it was, it was to be tested for strength and durability in a super-hot Timken furnace.

"They talked to a person later who was there that night and they said they couldn't cut it. They couldn't even heat it," said Sundi Multer-Lingle, Multer's daughter. She added, "The piece of metal—well, I don't know if you can call it metal, the object was absolutely impenetrable."[3]

One of the FBI agents made it very clear that not a word of the clandestine affair was to be spoken. Still, Multer would confide to his wife about, and starting in the 1960s would describe to his daughter, the day he "hauled material from the crashed spaceship." It became a well-kept secret within their family until Ralph passed away around 1990. It was then that Violet and Sundi spoke out publicly about the lightweight, metallic, silver-gray material that Timken couldn't dent, damage, or melt. His wife summarized, "The experience left a lasting impression on Ralph. It was always on his mind."[4]

What makes the previous information plausible is the story we are about to relate. Keep in mind that some of the crash debris allegedly arrived in Ohio via rail. We now return back to Roswell just outside the east gate—just before the train leaves the station.

As described earlier, the freight yard in Roswell in 1947 was just outside the east gate. For that reason it fell under the jurisdiction of the federal government under the authority of the civil service. The supervisor of that specific loading site was the late Charles Austin Wood, who is listed in the 1947 Roswell City Directory as a federal employee working for the civil service.[5]

Within days of all the talk about the crash of the flying saucer, Wood checked his morning freight assignments, which included a shipping car for the RAAF. No destination was given, and Wood would need to be present and then sign off that the cargo was loaded, secured, and en route to its next stopover. He noted the time and arrived earlier to ensure an available empty rail car.

At the predetermined time, a jeep of MPs raced across the tarmac proceeding toward the east gate. About 10 feet from the heavy wire-mesh fence, two of the guards leaped from the rear seat, and as one unlocked the padlock securing the gate, the other started to slide it along a metal channel, clearing a space for vehicles to drive through to the outside. Shortly thereafter, a truck followed, exited through the same opening, and arrived at the waiting freight car. The armed MPs next flanked the perimeter as the truck was directed as it backed toward the tracks. Wood continued to watch as soldiers began to take small wooden boxes from the rear cargo area of the truck and slide them into the waiting sidecar. An officer also watched and instructed the men's activity. The civil servant noted that the boxes were open at the top and appeared to contain pieces of jagged metal. Out of curiosity, Wood contemplated some plane mishap, but none had been reported in the local news. The base was typically very up-front with its civilian neighbors about such mishaps. But why all the security for mere wreckage? The pieces all looked the same from Wood's vantage point. And they sure didn't look like scraps from any aircraft or some weather balloon.[6]

One of those MPs was PFC Frank Vega, who, with five other men, was flown down to Roswell from Lowrey Army Air Field in Denver, Colorado. According to Vega, they were provided "grease guns" and assigned to guard Hangar P-3 with the orders "Don't ask any questions" and "Shoot to kill" any unauthorized individuals attempting to enter the hangar. Vega confirmed that the entire base was on "lockdown" and that he and his companions spent a full week, which included the loading of wreckage from the hangar being "loaded onto freight cars at the railroad spur."[7]

Frank Vega was given a "grease gun" and told to shoot on sight any unauthorized person trying to enter Hangar P-3 where the crash wreckage was stored, and he also helped to load wreckage onto railroad freight cars outside of the RAAF's east gate. Photo from 2012.

The workers were getting down to the last crate, and some of the enlisted men hopped back into the truck. Wood's curiosity continued and then something unexpected happened to reward his patience: As one of the last boxes was lifted into the car, a single remnant fell off the side of the container and dropped partially obscured under the boxcar. The soldier didn't seem to notice, as he crawled into the back of the truck just as the rear tailgate was slammed shut and ready to head back to the base. The project complete, the officer waved Wood over, and he scribbled his signature on the work order sheet without saying a word. And when they had all cleared the area and drove out of view back onto the base, Wood casually walked over to the now-closed freight car and stepped the orphaned piece of metal down into the dusty ground with his shoe. So far, so good. "Take the train away," shouted Wood to the engineer as he built up steam.

An abandoned railroad boxcar stands a lonely vigil on the rail spur near the Big Hangar on the old base at the spot where UFO crash wreckage was loaded in 1947 for transit "back east." Photo from 1998.

That night, as Roswell slept, Wood parked his car just outside the east gate of the base and slipped back to the train yard. The same remoteness and lack of human presence now served him well in his own recovery mission. After gaining his bearings and feeling around the ground in the dark, there it was: just beneath a thin layer of dirt. The orphan piece of metal now had a father by the name of Wood.[8]

Serviceman Frank Vega would tell us that after they completed the guard duty at the hangar, they "smelled like six skunks."[9] Rather than return to Lowrey, they were first sent to a closed base near Amarillo, Texas, where they would spend the next six months. They were not permitted to leave or have any outside communication during that entire "layover."[10] The entire Roswell affair needed to disappear, including the people who could talk.

Days would pass, then weeks, and after a few months it seemed like Wood had managed to accomplish what so many others had not. There were no strange visitors, no unexpected intruders, no one shadowing him. Charles Wood had in his possession something that could unravel the entire weather balloon resolution back to what started out to be one of the biggest stories of all time. All those witnesses like Vega, who only had memories of the true nature of the incident—and Wood had physical proof. But what to do with it? Tell the world or keep it secret. Readers will have to debate his decision.

Life in Roswell went on. Nevertheless, as the years passed, people still whispered among themselves. An air of lethargy remained within a community in which the high hopes for the post-war period were now tainted with suspicion and doubt. Wood wisely rode out the effects of living down the stigma of making claims that couldn't be proven. Still, he kept his confidence to himself. Not even his family knew what deep secrets he kept buried, as if still hidden out at the old freight yard.

The Woods' son, James, anxiously awaited the celebration of his sixth birthday in 1952. What could possibly be in the small box simply wrapped with no ribbon or bow? James could never have guessed, even after he opened the present and looked at it for what seemed like minutes waiting for his parents to tell him what it was. Charles asked, "Do you remember when I told you about all that excitement a few years ago when they thought a flying saucer crashed outside of Roswell? That's a piece of the weather balloon."[11] But James quickly realized that his dad was joking, because the more he bent it and crushed it and rolled it into a ball as his father instructed, it always smoothed out and back to its original shape. "Now watch this," Charles exclaimed. He then flicked his lighter and held the piece over the flame until it should have been black and very hot. Neither effect happened as the boy's eyes opened wider and wider. "Where did you get this?" For the first time he heard his father relate the experience back in 1947 loading up the freight car. "I thought they would have missed it by now," confessed Charles. "Now it's yours. Happy birthday, son."

James realized he had something none of his other school friends had. The very unlikelihood that he owned something from outer space both frightened him and energized him at the same time. And as the days passed, he felt all the more compelled to share it with his friends. But how to demonstrate it in all of its uniqueness? How to fully take advantage of highlighting its unearthly characteristics? Soon thereafter young James came up with a most novel solution.[12]

Like so many other boys of his age, James had a fascination with the art of magic and tried his hand at it. His father said that he and the other boys could use an old wooden shed as their clubhouse, which could also serve as James's little magician's parlor. And wouldn't you know he had the perfect finale for his routine.

Soon, little James Wood became the talk of his neighborhood. The little magician was drawing even adults to his act—as many that could fit into the old wooden shed. And each and every time, James would end his performance with the same climax: He would take the tissue-sized piece of metal from his folding table, display it to the audience, crumble it into a small ball, say some magic words, and finally toss it into the air. All were amazed to see it unravel and softly float to the ground. Applause, applause, as James quickly snatched up his star magic prop to secure it away for the next show.[13]

James Wood never let on how he acquired the strange metal with the magical abilities. He never said anything about where it was from. After all, magicians never reveal their secrets. Unfortunately for James, someone else was watching who decided the show needed to be cancelled. As one would predict, late one night, as everyone was sleeping and the clubhouse was locked for the night, someone else broke into the old wooden building and whisked away the physical evidence of a flying saucer crash. James had lost the best magic act a young boy could ever imagine. The Roswell police immediately suspected who the primary culprits were.[14] But like magicians, a government never reveals its secrets.

CHAPTER 10

Somebody's Watching You

*L*ittle did it ever occur to Mack Brazel that each and every new witness that he enlisted automatically became suspect. It was true that he had kept his own family out of the picture. Even 7-year-old Dee Proctor was not mentioned by Brazel to the authorities. And the deeper he realized he was sinking into a quagmire of sinister forces he had never encountered before, he maintained a level of his own suppression when it came to outing those he knew to be involved. It was only after the military conducted a systematic search and interrogation of just about all residents within a two-county area that specific measures were exerted contingent on the level of participation.

Geraldine Perkins ran a convenience store in Corona, New Mexico, in 1947. Photo from 2000.

According to the late Geraldine Perkins, who ran a small general store in Corona, which happened to have one of the only two telephones in town, Brazel used the phone to immediately contact his boss about his discovery.[1] The ranch that he supervised was owned by twin brothers, H.S. and J.B. Foster of Midland and Kent, Texas.

What has the Foster family maintained that crashed on their ranch in Lincoln County, New Mexico, for almost 70 years? For the next 16 years of Brazel's life, he remained convinced that what had deposited all that debris on the Foster ranch was a genuine flying saucer. And as for the likely possibility that his bosses merely accepted his word for it, the Foster family sped from Texas to New Mexico to investigate such an unbelievable claim. Unfortunately, they couldn't help Mack, and they couldn't walk away from the military, who would insist that the matter was of the utmost importance and required their full cooperation.

It was about 2001 when Cordy Derek confronted his grandfather, the son of H.S. Foster. The family called him "Papa," and up until that time he had always remained totally silent about what happened at the old Corona ranch. "He was totally evasive about the whole subject, and the way he behaved was unlike him," described Cordy.[2] It wasn't until Papa passed away in 2005 that his grandson took the opportunity to bring up the subject with his uncle. "I was 17 and working at the H.S. Foster ranch in Texas at the time of the crash. Those boys up there told me they were certain without a doubt that what they saw was a flying saucer," his uncle confessed. But when Cory asked him, "Did they see bodies?" his uncle stuttered, "Uh, uh…I can't remember. That's all I remember about that." Cory observed, "There was a certain gravity to his closing remark and the subject was never brought up again."

Shedding additional light on the involvement of the Foster family is the daughter of J.B. Foster, Jo Ann Purdie. She told us, "My dad knew it was a flying saucer and never changed his story. And just as the Army warned and threatened Mack Brazel, they did the same to him."[3] Purdie recalled how during the numerous times she accompanied her dad and they ran into Brazel after 1947, he refused to discuss the incident. "He would state that it wasn't any weather balloon," added Foster's daughter. She maintained that it would have been Brazel's responsibility to contact her father whenever there was any concern out at his New Mexican ranch. Clearly, by all of Brazel's behavior surrounding the affair, Foster would have been notified immediately long before Brazel contacted the authorities. Owning the property where the crash took place, the Fosters would have been in the forefront of the Army's concern. Purdie observed a stark change in the personality of her father after he returned home from New Mexico. "Whatever he saw or heard for himself, he didn't want to talk about it," said Purdie. "I have absolutely no doubt he believed all the threats, and they meant business," she somberly added.

When Mack's oldest son, Paul, learned about the trouble his father was in, he, too, drove over from his home in Texas. It was at the time that Mack was being detained and strong-armed by the Army at Roswell. Not having any ranch hands, at the least, Paul attempted to feed and water the penned horses on the Foster spread. "Every time I tried to get to the main ranch house [10 miles from the debris field] to water the horses in all that summer heat, the damn Army forced me off the ranch. I tried again the next day and they still threw me off the property. I was sure they did nothing for any of the animals," an angry Paul complained.[4]

"My dad was never the same," expressed Mack Brazel's son Bill, with a look of melancholy on his face. Possibly driven by emotion and being forced to quietly observe the ill treatment experienced by his father, Bill sought answers back at the location that set off the entire sordid affair. Especially after heavy rains, Bill would ride over the pasture seeking out pieces of physical evidence the military may have missed. He did this for his father—for the Brazel family. There would be no contact with the authorities, and it would remain a secret kept by just a handful of them: in the cigar box.[5]

Wife Shirley was especially entertained by the one piece of wreckage her husband Bill kept in his leather chaps. It was his favorite piece as well. Night after night as he would sit down to dinner after a hard day in the saddle working the ranch, he would reach into his pocket and the show would begin. Shirley served dinner but never bored at watching Bill try to cut or poke a hole through the piece with his "buck" knife. It was somewhat shiny on one side, duller on the other, and about the size of a handkerchief. And each night before Bill would start eating, he would provide one last demonstration: No matter how he mangled the metal-like piece, he placed it on the dinner table and it always smoothed out into its original condition. Amazing.[6]

Bill Brazel kept in a cigar box a few "scraps of metal" from the 1947 crash that he found on the Foster ranch, only to have them confiscated by the military two years later. Photo from 1998.

One sunny day, Bill had a bad case of human nature and just had to show his secret piece to someone else. Sally Tadolini was the daughter of Lyman and Marian Strickland, one of Brazel's neighbors. Pulling up to the ranch house, Sally happened to be outside, and Bill showed her his prized-possession. According to Tadolini, he first displayed the piece, then "balled it up in his hand, and when he opened his hand it just smoothed right out." She added, "my immediate impression was, 'Oh my. Wouldn't it be wonderful if clothes were made of such material? I'd never have to iron again.'"[7] From a human perspective, this paints a nice visual picture.

It was something Bill regretted the rest of his life—the day he gave into the same intimidation as his father had suffered. What innocently began as an evening of playing some billiards and downing a few with fellow ranchers at Wade's Bar in Corona caused the

Brazel family to once again place themselves in the government's crosshairs. "Say, Bill. Did anyone ever find any more pieces from that crash which got everyone so excited?" asked one of the patrons. "Well, I did find a few scraps," quipped Bill with a tad look of mischievousness in his eye. But that's all he would say on the matter. And he left for the hour drive back to the ranch.

After everything that had befallen his family since the incident, what happened early the next morning even surprised Bill. Who should be at his door but Air Force Captain Emerson Armstrong and three non-commissioned officers (NCOs). "Mr. Brazel," stated the officer, "You have something we want and you will give it to us." In post–WWII America, the military walked on water, and Bill found himself retrieving each of the recovered artifacts he thought were his to keep. That is unless someone was watching—listening. He had slipped up, and he knew it as he handed over the brimming cigar box. Armstrong was surprised that it was more than just a "few scraps," and earnestly suggested that Brazel lead them out to the general area where he had gathered his treasure.[8] With three more sets of eyes, they needed to be sure that Brazel couldn't start a new collection after they departed.

While her father was leading Armstrong and the others out to pasture, Fawn (Fritz) and her mother, Shirley, were left alone to experience the second wave. According to Fawn, "There were six more soldiers, three of whom came right into the house. They pulled drawers from a dresser, emptied a closet and pried up some loose floorboards. They completely trashed our house."[9] The others were inspecting the cattle shed located about sixty feet from the house. "[They] started to slit open each feedbag and let it pour out over the ground," she went on to describe. "They even emptied a water holding tank!" she exclaimed. Evidently, the Air Force was not taking this situation too lightly. Some would say that these actions smacked of paranoia, as though they feared some dark secret spilling out.

Their behavior would only amplify the growing intensity of the situation. Flying saucers were an unexpected phenomenon. Civilian witnesses stumbling about still securing proof that could expose the cover-up complicated matters. It was as though the Great War still continued. Nonetheless, both sides were still stumbling in the dark. No one had any answers, and both sides grew impatient. After all, the year that Captain Armstrong and his group of marauders raided the home of Bill Brazel was 1949—two years after the incident. Two years of searching for answers. Two years of watching....

Fawn Fritz, Mack Brazel's granddaughter, described for the authors how the military ransacked their ranch house and cattle shed, and cut open feed bags searching for pieces of UFO crash wreckage. Photo from 2006.

"Typically, after heavy rains up in the Lincoln County region, that's when they'd make their move," commented Major Charles A. McGee.[10] The officer was a sentry on the west gate of the base—which literally led to nothing. Yet, according to McGee, the only thing the gate was ever used for was base personnel secretly bypassing the city of Roswell and then heading north using other roads. Destination: the debris field. Men would slip out from this unoccupied area of the base proper and rendezvous with accomplices pulling horse trailers. Then they'd change into ranch attire and inconspicuously ride through the wreckage site on horseback, scouring the ground for any missed remnants form the crash.

More than 50 years after this clandestine activity, McGee still expressed amazement: "This went on for about two and a half years!"[11] Adding further corroboration to this testimony was none other than Walter Haut, who stated, "They were still searching the desert for a couple of years after the crash."[12] Clearly, Bill Brazel's shocking experience two years after the original, full-scale recovery operation demonstrates the ongoing concern the military has displayed in retrieving any evidence contrary to the official balloon explanation—even if it should take years.

When Tech Sergeant Steven Akins was instructed to check a vehicle out of the motor pool at Cannon Air Force Base in April 1986, he never imagined it would take him back to 1947. The base is located in Clovis, New Mexico, just an hour northeast of Roswell. Two officers arrived from Washington, and he was to drive them to an undisclosed location. No other information was given. At first they headed to Roswell, had lunch, and then drove into Lincoln County to the northwest. Later, it became clear to Akins that they needed Roswell as a launching point. One officer was a lieutenant colonel, and he and the other officer kept referring to maps. First they passed through Carrizozo, next north to Corona, and then, according to Akins, "We drove out from Corona on Highway 247. The one officer sitting in the back seat kept busy in his brief case and appeared to refer to some directional notes. We drove quite a few miles before turning south on a dirt road. At one point we came to a fork, incorrectly veered left, was told to back up, and then continued southeast."[13] The terrain became rougher and Akins became more concerned about breaking down out in the "middle of nowhere." Finally, the one officer instructed Akins to stop and the two strangers got out. "They stayed together as they walked the vacant pasture, looking for who knows what. The area was extremely rough and they paid special attention at the base of a bluff. I did recognize the Capitan Mountains to our west," added the enlisted man. After some time passed, the officers returned to the waiting Akins and told him to return them to the base, retracing the original route. Their driver couldn't help but grow in curiosity until he finally blurted out, "What's this all about?" The lieutenant colonel said non-descriptly, "[P]art of a UFO," supposedly crashed at that location. As much as Akins wanted to pepper them with more questions, it became immediately evident that neither officer had anything else to comment. Not another word was exchanged for the balance of the peculiar mission. Hours later, upon their return to Cannon, the lieutenant colonel took Akins aside and stated that the drive and the comment he made were "guarded information."

As ranch hand James Parker approached the trespassers, the words "U.S. Air Force" jumped from their pickup's door like a flash-ing neon sign. It was October 1987, and inside the vehicle, with topo-graphical maps scattered on the dash and console between them, sat two middle-aged men. The driver, a corporal, and his private first class partner, looked rather out of "true" uniform due to their ages. This is a common ploy by military officers to avoid detection when conducting undercover field work: appear like underlings just out for a sight-seeing adventure. Nevertheless, they were still on private property. "Get the hell off of this land!" ordered Parker.[14] Neither of the two interlopers volunteered identification. Ranch hand Parker had no idea where they were from or who sent them. The driver stammered as he attempted to explain the awkward situation by offering the silly notion of checking out the final location for a "low-altitude radar tracking facility" for monitoring drug smugglers fly-ing in from Mexico. Parker had no idea what he was spouting. His foreman, Jeff Wells, had never mentioned any such arrangement with the authorities. There is no such tracking system anywhere in New Mexico. That being said, a loaded Winchester rifle pointed in the face of the driver ended any such debate, and the Air Force was forced to retreat. Before driving off the "corporal" did have one last question: "By the way, you saw where we were originally coming from. Is that where that 'flying saucer' crashed back in 1947?" This scenario was 40 years later, in the fall of 1987. From the moment Parker was hired, no one had ever mentioned the significance of that very ranch. As far as he was concerned, the two strangers just made their trespassing even more ridiculous. "Get moving now!"

A vast assortment of physical proof was confiscated from more civilians than we will ever know. Some may have temporarily slipped through the official grasp of the U.S. military, but, though we have had numerous false alarms, no such evidence has ever surfaced to us and no one is talking. Accounts of home and vehicle intrusions abound even up to the 1980s, and so do the mysterious disappearances of actual debris. The question remains: If Roswell involved the mere recovery of a Mogul balloon comprised of off-the-shelf materials, why have the arbiters of that same steadfast explanation made sure that the real physical evidence has never been exposed? Why is the actual debris, which would appear to include the original debris field, the principal motivation for the continuing surveillance—the continuing watching? And wouldn't it be to their advantage if any of the very possessors of such physical evidence were permitted to display a piece of mundane, conventional material, that is, if indeed the real material would support their official contention? Their actions would suggest otherwise—even at the risk of having a Winchester pointed in their faces.

CHAPTER 11

As the Air Force's Wooden Nose Grows

The greatest irony of the military's treatment of the Roswell Incident is that the specific branch now held responsible for the case is the Air Force—when it didn't even exist in July 1947. Roswell was an Army affair. True, the actual creation and breaking off by the Air Force took place over the six months after the crash. And Roswell Army Air Field became Walker Air Field in January 1948. Nevertheless, the Air Force will forever be associated with the official investigation of the UFO enigma and occasionally makes pronouncements on the topic today, albeit on general terms and always with a rather dismissive sweep of the hand. Roswell remains the only alleged UFO case that has been singled out by the Air Force, and forced it to actually investigate an alternative explanation, prepare an extensive report, and then have a succession of press conferences at the Pentagon. Clearly, as the mounting pressure from New Mexico Congressman Steven Schiff began to draw more attention to the "Air Force's" bumbling lack of cooperation for his mere request for their files on the matter, it saw the urgent need to respond. Not with files from 1947, but rather with modern-day accumulated files from a new cover story developed in 1993. As *Newsweek* magazine very aptly put it in July 1994, "In an attempt to preempt the GAO, [failing cooperation from the Air Force, the General Accounting Office was asked by Schiff to conduct a records search on the Roswell Incident] the Air Force released their own report on Roswell."[1] The 32-page internal investigation, *Report of Air Force Research Regarding the Roswell Incident,* "theorized" that the crash debris could be explained away as a balloon train from a continuing series of high-altitude test instruments deployed to detect the sound wave of the impending first Soviet nuclear detonation. Unfortunately, for the Air Force, just as with the previous Rawin weather balloon, which served as its official explanation up until that time, this Project Mogul test balloon was almost entirely assembled with the same "off-the-shelf" materials that anyone would have readily identified. And besides, none of the launch dates coincided with the crash discovery, and none of the witnesses have ever claimed it was a balloon or anything else just as conventional.

In September 1995, the Air Force released a 1,000-page monograph entitled *The Roswell Report: Fact vs. Fiction in the New Mexico Desert.* This was after it officially stated in the previous report that *that* would be its final word on the subject of the Roswell Incident. This particular overblown fluff piece attempted to further explain the crash as a result of a downed Mogul instrument package, with about 950 additional pages that laid out in laborious detail every other possible launch, test, and crash of just about everything else thrown in for good measure. No evidence, no witnesses, just their new "theory." And like the original balloon explanation from 1947, the press bowed down and fully accepted this "third" official solution to the strange unearthly wreckage described by dozens of witnesses. But wait—they weren't yet through with Roswell: What about all the accounts that mentioned "little people"?

As long as the rumors of recovered bodies at Roswell remained, the Air Force realized that it hadn't dumped the final shovel of ground on the coffin. And almost as quickly as the architects of the Mogul explanation breathed a sigh of relief, as the press heaved their own shovel, they next lept at the opportunity to take the entire case down once and for all. Congressman Schiff wasn't buying the new story. His constituents were holding fast to their original stories and the clock had yet to run out. As long as witnesses were still around to challenge the Air Force version of events, the battle wasn't over. What was worse, the 50th anniversary of the incident was looming, which would once again elevate the story in the international news. Another pre-emptive strike was necessary. But what the Pentagon decided to do was not only inaccurate, but outright laughable.

In June 1997, the headquarters of the United States Air Force published *The Roswell Report: Case Closed*. The timely report was authored by Captain James McAndrew, who had coauthored the Mogul report with Colonel Richard L. Weaver three years before. What should be pointed out is that McAndrew was a "Reserve" Intelligence Applications Officer. In 1993 he had been reactivated and assigned to the Secretary of the Air Force Declassification and Review Team at the Pentagon. One should question why the Air Force felt the need to bring in a non-active officer, but secondly, and more importantly, a lower-rank officer who hardly would have access to classified files.

The new report, not only intended to reinforce the previous Mogul explanation, also provided the following conclusions:

∠ Air Force activities that occurred over a period of many years have been consolidated and are now represented to have occurred in two or three days.

∠ "Aliens" observed in the New Mexico desert were probably anthropomorphic test dummies that were carried aloft by U.S. Air Force high-altitude balloons for scientific research.

∠ The "unusual" military activities in the New Mexico desert were high-altitude research balloon launch and recovery operations. The reports of military units that always seemed to arrive shortly after the crash of a flying saucer to retrieve the saucer and "crew" were actually accurate descriptions of Air Force personnel engaged in anthropomorphic dummy recovery operations.

Captain McAndrew was assigned to come up with an answer to all of the continuing accounts about bodies recovered at Roswell, and as a duly assigned officer of the U.S. Air Force, he failed miserably.

It was in June 1943 that a young officer jumped from an aircraft at an astounding altitude of 40,200 feet. The sudden lurch as his parachute opened caused him to black out, and the initial speed of decent had ripped off one of his protective gloves, which resulted in frostbite to his hands. William Randolph "Randy" Lovelace II was a physician specializing in aerospace medicine and the study of high-altitude flight. The Aero Medical Laboratory at Wright Field in Dayton, Ohio, had assigned Lovelace to develop an oxygen mask for use in extreme-altitude aircraft. Experimenting with high-altitude parachutes, Lovelace was most fortunate to have only suffered frost-bite when he made such a high-risk jump in 1943.[2]

As though in reverse order of test progression, monkeys were next used in similar tests, with mostly fatal results. The poor animals would often freeze solid and at times shatter into pieces upon impacting the ground. Nevertheless, the research was inconclusive and the Air Force saw the necessity of pursuing its original agenda. Herein lays one of the connections to Roswell.

Since the final year of WWII (1945), the Air Material Command headquartered at Wright Field started to experiment with rope and sandbag dummies as best they could re-create the size, shape, and weight of a human being. In an attempt to expand the project to provide the needs in experiments to include measuring the effect of rapid acceleration and deceleration during high-speed pilot ejection, a human replica that could wear an aviation helmet, oxygen mask, and pressure uniform with pilot safety harness was designed. The Anthropology Branch of the Aero Medical Laboratory at Wright Field was responsible for the final design.[3]

So, in 1952, a full five years after the Roswell Incident, Alderson Research Laboratories of New York City was contracted to produce a 6-foot tall, 200-pound anthropomorphic dummy. It was constructed of latex or plastic skin encasing a metal frame of either steel or aluminum, along with a cast aluminum head and instrument packages that fit into the torso and skull. While fully hinged and jointed at the extremities, it had no pelvic structure and little spinal articulation. Such dummies were dropped over New Mexico with parachutes or ejection seats starting in 1953 under the project names "High Dive" and "Excelsior." And as unbelievable as it may sound, the U.S. Air Force in 1997 concluded that, "Dummies of these types were most likely the 'aliens' associated with the 'Roswell Incident,'" which happened in 1947![4]

Physicist and engineer Samuel W. Alderson, a true pioneer in biomechanics, is credited with inventing the first crash dummies. He is also credited with having created the "aliens" seen at Roswell— that is, by the Air Force. A rather dubious honor considering that during WWII he assisted in new submarine periscope technology, as well as depth charge and missile guidance system instrumentation. Alderson also created "medical phantoms," which could demonstrate radiation exposure as well as open battlefield wounds. All of this was tremendously advantageous for emergency simulation training. Not bad for a former doctoral student of J. Robert Oppenheimer and Ernest O. Lawrence.[5] And still, the Air Force, specifically Captain McAndrew, singled out Alderson as the source of all the accounts of "bodies" at Roswell.

When the Pentagon presented its fourth explanation of Roswell just weeks before the 50th anniversary of the now-famous event, Alderson was watching from his home in California—and he was outraged.[6]

Aside from manufacturing human surrogates for the Air Force, he was also contracted by NASA to design space capsule safety systems. As a result, he traveled extensively in high-ranking Air Force circles as well as with some of the most respected scientific consultants working with the newly established space program. According to his son, Jeremy, on two occasions his father was shown specific evidence that convinced him of the reality of the flying saucers. One was an officer who served as an investigator of such reports, and the other a military pilot. Alderson was left with no doubt suggesting the level of the sources.[7]

Aside from the unexplainable six-year time discrepancy between the actual year of the Roswell event and the first dropping of the test dummies, Alderson pointed out to his son details that McAndrew merely mentioned in his "Case Closed" report. For example, not only did Alderson Labs construct the dummies, they maintained and prepped each one for each new use. Here is where Alderson was especially agitated by the government suggesting that his dummies were the aliens seen at the time of the Roswell Incident. Not a single witness to the actual event has ever described any dismemberment of the bodies. No scattered limbs, no arms or legs missing: Bodies, from their perspective, were entirely intact—whereas the test-dummies had to be continuously repaired and reassembled. After each test drop and the subsequent impact with all sorts of rough terrain out in the New Mexican desert, "They broke up with pieces flying in all directions," according to what Alderson described to his son Jeremy[8]: "Even if the crash happened in 1953, their size alone would have disqualified them as any likely candidate. After each drop, we literally had to put them back together again." Jeremy told us that his father went to his grave in 2005 knowing that his creations "had absolutely nothing to do with Roswell." As he was near death, his son showed him a DVD about UFOs, which turned out to be totally skeptical. Within moments, his father turned it off, saying, "I refuse to waste my time watching something that is nothing more than an attempt to refute the truth."

Earlier in 1947, months before the crash of the craft of unknown origin, retired colonel, now doctor, Randy Lovelace helped establish the Lovelace Medical Foundation in Albuquerque, New Mexico. The new facility was to specialize in medical aerospace technology, and Lovelace would eventually become the chairman of NASA's Special Advisory Committee on Life Science and before his death its director of space medicine.[9]

One of the primary research areas being tested in 1947 was the effect of radiation and biological warfare on primates, rodents, and dogs. Specific areas of concern were lung cancer and emphysema.[10] As a result of Lovelace's proximity to Roswell and his medical expertise, we had long heard rumors of his being involved in the incident. Then, in 2011 we had the good fortune to meet with neurosurgeon Dr. Mark D. Erasmus of the Presbyterian Medical Clinic of Albuquerque, who informed us that years before he had worked with a nurse who worked with Lovelace back in 1947. According to the nurse, her boss was indeed quickly dispatched to Roswell at the same time as all the press coverage. He did not return for a couple of days and when he did, unlike other assignments, he refused to comment on what he knew. The only confession the nurse heard come from the lips of Dr. Randy Lovelace was that he had "gone to Roswell" and "[it]...was a new species."[11]

You will not read the nurse's story in any newspaper, but nonetheless, she is a heroine. She worked at Wright-Patterson AFB as a

Top Secret stenographer from 1942 through 1953. And she just happened to be there when a "close friend," an army sergeant, displayed parts of a "spaceship" from New Mexico that had just crashed.[12] That same friend almost lost control when he described the bodies he had also witnessed.

June Crain was a stenographer at Wright-Patterson AFB in Dayton, Ohio, holding a Q clearance, which permitted her to handle documents and hear discussions regarding UFOs. Early 1950s photo.

But that is not what made this remarkable woman special and someone whose testimony should be beyond reproach. What made June Crain a true heroine was her lifelong battle with cancer, her being responsible for the apprehension of a spy and receiving a special commendation, and most of all her personal fortitude to go on after she had lost her husband and one of her children in a terrible car accident. She still started her own business, which was very successful in providing affordable housing for the poor. Then she helped to raise the needed funding to construct her town's first public library. And through it all, this American patriot managed to maintain her silence for 40 years about what she knew to be the truth about Roswell. Fortunately for us, all of that changed when the Air Force released the insulting crash dummy report. In June 1997 told herself she had had enough of the lies. She finally came forward and told what really happened, including how one of the scientists at Wright-Patterson was laughing out loud about the press falling for the balloon cover story, and how she had personally tried to cut, tear, and bend the weightless material she was shown from the crash, to no effect.[13] Sadly, you won't read any of the actual eyewitnesses' accounts in the press—only the government version of what officialdom wants us to believe.

Immediately after the crash dummy report was released, we pointed out to the Pentagon that most all of the witnesses we had to the bodies were no longer in New Mexico in 1953 or thereafter, which would disqualify them from mistakenly identifying manufactured dummies as biological bodies of any sort. We also explained how, contrary to claims in the Air Force report, many of our witnesses discussed the bodies with their families long before 1980 when the first book about Roswell, *The Roswell Incident,* was published. But allow us to state for the record that Captain McAndrew never spoke with a single one of our witnesses before completing his report; he never spoke to us, either. Still the new explanation was a major victory in our eyes: For the first time, the U.S. Air Force conceded some form of bodies were recovered at

Crash-test dummies like the one being supported by two airmen in the photo were employed in the mid- to late 1950s in high-altitude parachute drop tests in advance of the nascent U.S. space program.

Roswell. And as best as it tried, the closest it could come to anything out of the ordinary was six years removed. One might speculate, if it had to focus strictly on 1947, what might the Air Force have been forced to consider? And we might add that we're sure, just as the Air Force knows, they were not any type of crash dummies. Samuel Alderson, Randy Lovelace, June Crain, and all the witnesses at Roswell know they weren't. We believe Captain McAndrew also knows. Not that we believe he has ever had access to the truth, but we would credit him with being intelligent enough to know that his closing arguments do not even correspond with 1947—a fact that would disqualify his report in any court of law. Case dismissed.

CHAPTER 12

A Roswell Favorite Son Makes Good, But Also Remembers...

After it happened, the town was never the same again.

—Tom Brookshier

*T*he caustically crusty, yet somehow friendly, voice leaving a message on the answering machine could only be one person. "Hey, Carey! Whaddya mean I couldn't cover Renfro? What game were you watchin'? You don't know what you're talkin' about."[1] The caller was referring to the former Cleveland Browns' crafty wide receiver, Ray Renfro, and a deliberately provocative allegation planted by co-author Tom Carey on the caller's answering machine that might ignite him to return Carey's call. It worked to a "T."

Thomas Jefferson "Brookie" Brookshier (pronounced "BROOK-shrr" by locals in his hometown of Roswell, New Mexico) was an all-pro defensive cornerback for the Philadelphia Eagles of the National Football League when his career ended abruptly on a sunny October afternoon in 1961 at Philadelphia's venerable Franklin Field in a game between the then-defending NFL champion Eagles and the visiting Chicago Bears. Brookshier, noted for his fierce tackling, was coming up to meet the Bears' speedy and shifty halfback, Willie Galimore, near the sideline where the Bears' bench was when his leg collided with Galimore's leg at the same time it was struck from behind by another player's leg in a "whipsaw" fashion. The result was a compound fracture of Brookshier's right shinbone (tibia). His nascent NFL "Hall of Fame" career was over at age 30. The Bears' iconic coach George Halas, no doubt realizing the gravity of the situation for the stricken player on the ground in front of him, offered a short lament to the fallen warrior, one that famed former Notre Dame coach Knute Rockne himself might have give: "Tough break, Kid."[2]

In the 1950s there was a popular weekly TV series entitled *I Led Three Lives*, which was the true story about (1) an ordinary American citizen, "Herbert Philbrick," played by character actor Richard Carlson (*It Came From Outer Space, Riders to the Stars, Creature From the Black Lagoon*), who also posed as (2) a card-carrying member of the CPUSA (Communist Party of the USA) and, most importantly, (3) was a counter-spy for the FBI.

Looking back over Tom Brookshier's life story for this book, the same trifecta could equally be said of him, but not all occurring at the same time. First and foremost, he was an outstanding, three-sport athlete in his youth, receiving All-State honors in high school in baseball, football, and basketball. By the time he entered the University of Colorado in the fall of 1949, he had settled mostly on football and made a few All-American rosters as a fullback, kick returner, and defensive back. He was also a relief pitcher on the baseball team, but although he struck out a lot of batters, he walked even more. As one teammate remarked, "He [Brookshier] had a really good fastball, but he just never knew where it was going."[3] His future course of action, however, was decided for him when the Philadelphia Eagles selected him in the 10th round (117th player chosen) of the 1953 NFL draft.

For someone hailing from a town—Roswell, New Mexico, sometimes referred to as being "West of Nowhere and South of Lost"— Tom Brookshier would have been successful wherever he was from and whatever he did in life. It's not surprising, then, that he should garner a roomful of athletic, broadcasting, and civic awards to put on his shelves for posterity. Starting out as a three-sport, All-State athlete in his native New Mexico, he went on to a Hall of Fame athletic career at the University of Colorado, followed by inductions into the Pennsylvania Hall of Fame, the Philadelphia Eagles All-Time Honor Roll, and the Broadcast Pioneers of Philadelphia Hall of Fame. He also received numerous awards of distinction, including the Bert Bell Award, the Washington Touchdown Club's Outstanding Broadcaster Award, the Philadelphia Sports Writers Association Award, and Emmy Awards for Outstanding Live Sports Series.[4] Brookshier's Eagles #40 jersey was retired in 1962, never to be worn again—only the fourth Eagle to be so honored up to that time. (There are now nine.)

In the summer of 1947, Tommie Brookshier, one of five children, was on summer vacation from school.[5] He was 15 years old. When he was not playing baseball, he was pumping gas at his father's service station, located on North Main Street in Roswell. A result of these "extracurricular" activities, especially the latter, was that the gregarious young Brookshier got to know a number of the airmen from the airbase just south of town.

In July 2008, co-author Tom Carey and his wife, Doreen, were in Roswell for the town's yearly UFO festival. Tom and co-author Don Schmitt have been annual speakers at the International UFO Museum during the festival there since the early 1990s. On the day before the start of the festivities, Tom decided to show Doreen some of the sights of Roswell. While walking the grounds of Roswell's famous New Mexico Military Institute (NMMI), a military-style high school that includes famous newsman Sam Donaldson, Academy Award–winning motion picture actor Joel McCrea, and NFL Hall of Fame quarterback Roger Staubach among its graduates, they came upon the school's football stadium. Tom, a former three-sport athlete himself, stopped at the open end of the empty stadium to take in the view of the green grass on the field, the goal posts, and the rows of empty seats, while Doreen continued walking on. A minute or two later, the silence was broken by Doreen's voice: "Tom! Over here!" She was looking at a bronze plaque with a dozen or so names embossed on it. Tom immediately recognized most of the names on the plaque as those of pro football players, past and current. Why were their names on that plaque?

Reading further, the plaque identified the names etched on it as players who played at least one football game on the hallowed turf of NMMI stadium and then had gone on to play pro football. Roger Staubach's name jumped out at once, but one other name on the plaque caught Tom's attention: the name "Tom Brookshier."

Tom Carey knew all about Tom Brookshier as a former Philadelphia Eagles player as well as a TV and radio sports broadcaster and personality, but in 2008 he did not know that Brookshier hailed from Roswell, New Mexico. Doing some quick arithmetic in his head, Carey calculated that Brookshier had been a teenager at the time of the Roswell UFO Incident of July 1947. He immediately filed it away in his mental "to-do basket" to try to interview Brookshier when he returned home after the festival.

Brookshier told Carey over the phone:

Yes, I do remember when that happened. I was a typical male teenager then, interested mostly in sports and girls, but I also knew a lot of guys from the base because they all used to stop at my father's filling station, where I worked a lot, for gas. I remember that when the UFO incident happened back in '47, the base was closed down for about a week to outsiders as if a curtain had been dropped around it. After it was lifted, the guys I knew from the base became very distant and didn't want to talk to me anymore when they came in for gas. It was all very strange to me, because I was just a kid at the time. But to my mind in retrospect, the relationship between the base and the town of Roswell was never the same again after that.[6]

He remembered that, at the time of the incident, a reporter had approached him and some of his friends asking about the "flying saucer." Instead of answering the reporter's question in a serious way, the boys made a joke out of it by asking the reporter if the "flying saucer" had crashed into Carlsbad High School, 77 miles south of Roswell, which was a football rival of Brookshier's own team, the Roswell High School Coyotes. If it hadn't crashed or hit any of the Carlsbad football players, then they wouldn't be interested in the "aliens," they told the reporter. Just so the reporter understood where Brookshier and his buddies' minds were, and that the reporter was wasting his time by interviewing them, Brookshier offered one final nugget: "Unless they [the aliens] are good football players and can help us whip Carlsbad, we don't think about them [the aliens] too much."[7]

Carey pressed Brookshier for information about what he knew firsthand about the 1947 UFO incident and what he might have also heard secondhand about it. Brookshier explained that he only had one additional firsthand encounter relating to the incident beyond the closing of the base and its aftermath and his run-in with the reporter. He had heard a number of stories about people he had known who were involved on a firsthand basis, one way or another.

Several weeks after the incident, Brookshier was talking to some of his friends when one interjected, "Has anybody here seen what Roy Tyner has? You ought to see it. It's like nothing like you've ever seen before!"[8] Roy Tyner was a Roswell welder who had a shop on E. 2nd Street in town. The young Brookshier knew him through Tyner's kids and his father's service station. The story sounded too weird for the boys to pass up. So they all trekked over to Tyner's shop to have a look for themselves. Tyner was working, but the boys harassed him to the point where he had to show them what they had come to see. Tyner put down his torch and walked over to his greasy work desk and opened one of the drawers. He then pulled out something from the drawer and wadded it up in his hand, and walked back over to where the boys were standing. "Watch this," he told them. With his fist clenched, he held his right arm straight out at shoulder level and then opened his fist. Out unfurled a very thin piece of aluminum-colored *something* that looked like metal. But instead of falling to the floor of Tyner's shop like the boys expected, it just stayed there, floating in mid-air where Tyner had released it! "Seen enough, boys?" Tyner asked them. "Now get out of here." Before they left, one of boys asked Tyner where he had gotten it. "From the flying saucer crash, now get out of here." How Tyner had come by the strange piece of metal was never explained. But Brookshier told Carey that it was one of the strangest things he'd ever seen in his life.

Shortly thereafter, Carey interviewed Roy Tyner's widow, Jo, who confirmed that her husband had indeed possessed a "piece of the wreckage" from the UFO crash. She also revealed that at some point he hid the piece under the seat in his pickup truck for a couple of years. Then, when he sold the truck, he had apparently forgotten about it. She recalled:

> Then, sometime later, I saw him madly looking around the house for something with a wild look on his face. "Where is it?" he kept saying. "Where's what?" I said. "The piece from the flying saucer." I told him that he had last kept it in his truck, and out the door he ran like a madman with a wild look on his face. Well, he found the truck somewhere all right, but the piece was gone. To this day, no one knows what happened to it.[9]

Tom Brookshier may have also provided us with the key clue from a secondhand account of his that may finally help us solve the long sought-after "nurse" who was at the heart of a story told for years by Roswell mortician, the late Glenn Dennis.[10] Thanks to Tom Brookshier, we now believe that we know the name of the nurse who was actually involved in the aborted alien autopsy out at the

Roswell base hospital and, just as important, how Dennis learned the details of her story and adopted it as his own. This particular investigation is still not concluded. So, we must leave it there for the present to preserve its integrity.

By the end of Carey's interview with Tom Brookshier, Carey felt that he had made a new friend. Even though "Brookie" had never met Carey or even heard of him, it was like two old friends talking on the phone. Carey had always planned to meet with Brookshier in person to record a videotaped interview. The unexpected passing of this true sports legend unfortunately obviated those plans. No one in the public domain knew that Brookshier was even sick. Diagnosed with a virulent form of gall bladder cancer in July 2009, Philadelphia's beloved "Brookie" was gone six months later.

Testimonials and remembrances came from all over the sports world on the passing of the Eagles' #40. *Philadelphia Inquirer* sports writer Bill Lyon perhaps said it best with this succinct statement: "He was 78, and what he leaves behind is 78 years' worth of smiles. Can there be a better legacy?"[11]

Maybe Tom Brookshier was just too young in 1947 to comprehend the importance of what was then taking place in and around the town of Roswell early that summer. Maybe he was just being a typical teenage boy interested in teenage boy things: sports, fast and loud cars, and girls. In what order, we will never know. One thing we know for sure, however, is that the 1947 incident did not seem to affect his affable personality, his optimistic wit, or his chosen career paths in any negative way. When interviewed by Carey, he remembered the 1947 incident, but in recalling it, it was clear that he hadn't given much thought to it over the years.[12] That was his nature. He saw a potential, humorous quip in everyone and everything he encountered, and most likely that is how he handled the potential "visitors from space" issue suggested by the Roswell Incident.

Once, some years ago while broadcasting an NFL Game of the Week, there was a stir among the large crowd in the stands. They were all pointing skyward at something strange that was spinning like a top over the stadium where the game was being played. The TV camera panned to look at it, and it did look strange indeed, but as usual Brookshier captured the on-air moment with a succinct, effacing-but-humorous remark: "Take me to your leader!"[13] Little did we know then, but now we understand. We understand. RIP, Tom.

CHAPTER 13

"They Sure Weren't From Texas"

Please allow us to take exception to the overall theme of this book. We are about to recount the story of a "child" of Roswell of a different sort. His involvement, unlike all the other participants related in this tome, was not that of a family member, though his entire family would become enveloped in many aspects of the affair. But his mission was unique, and he played out his central role in the Roswell Incident aftermath right up until his passing. The true nature of his "role-playing" would not emerge until sometime after that.

During our very first visit to New Mexico in February 1989, we sought out the very public information officer from the old Roswell Army Air Field (RAAF) from 1947: Walter G. Haut. Walter, who was born and raised in Chicago, was one of a handful of former military assigned to Roswell who elected to stay, raise their families, and eventually stay in Roswell for the balance of their lives. We have addressed Walter's participation in the original event previously (see Chapter 4); for now we will focus on how he led us to a most intriguing gentleman who would turn the very concept of our investigation on its head.

As mentioned, Walter Haut remained in Roswell after he unexpectedly resigned from the Army just a little more than a year after the 1947 event. As he took up a civilian lifestyle in his new chosen community, first he sold insurance, and then he opened up an art gallery, which he operated for the next 15 years. As a result of his local business affiliation in Roswell, it was in his best interest to nurture relationships with the chamber of commerce—specifically its acting president. Along with their spouses, the two men became good business associates as well as close personal friends. Often, they would enjoy the company of one another over dinner and, more often, drinks. Their mutual years at the old RAAF base were distant memories, and Walter had no idea that his friend was hiding a secret history of his own. And it would shock Walter to the termination of their longtime friendship.

It was at one of the annual 509th Squadron reunions at the now-gone Roswell Inn motel that Walter overheard his friend make specific remarks about something never shared with him. As the executive vice president of the Roswell Chamber of Commerce tipped a few drinks with a number of old Army buddies in the motel lounge, he made specific recollections about personal knowledge of the 1947 incident. At the time, Walter assumed it was just casual discussion and tended to his own affairs. After all, if it wasn't important enough to ever mention in private, how relevant could it be? How relevant indeed.

From the very first time we had the pleasure of meeting Walter Haut, and for most of the balance of his life, he made every effort to remain the outsider with regard to his 1947 involvement. This was one of the reasons from early on that he constantly diverted attention from himself, but rather to other potential witnesses who might be able to provide us with information. It was no surprise that he eventually called to our attention the individual he had overheard at the reunion just a few years before. Nevertheless, as we would immediately discover, such an endorsement was made by a friend and fellow businessman. It had absolutely nothing to do with anything related to the crash of the "flying saucer." Like us, Walter was about to hear just how much he didn't know about his post-military friend.

"Unpack, honey. We're staying in Roswell," exclaimed Frank as he came in from the garage. "What are you talking about?" his puzzled wife, Juanita, asked. "I just got a job with the chamber of commerce, so we can start unpacking," her husband described as he grabbed the phone to start putting out their unexpected change of plans. Juanita noted that Frank was just as surprised as she was.[1]

Frank J. Kaufmann was born in New York City on March 1, 1916. After high school he attended business college for one and a half years, taking courses in administration and management, then spent one year at New York University taking classes in advertising and social arts. Lastly, he attended the New York Academy of Fine Arts for the following two years, where he demonstrated an artistic talent for landscapes. Frank was truly gifted as an artist, and his many beautiful paintings attest to that fact.

From August 5, 1942, until October 30, 1945, he served in the U.S. Army and was honorably discharged with the rank of Staff Sergeant. His last assignment was at the Roswell Army Air Field. From all his available military records, Frank had a stellar office career, albeit a short one with the military. And for that reason, he was asked to continue serving at the base, but in a civilian capacity, and he was clearly there at the time of the events of 1947. Enter Frank J. Kaufmann—Roswell witness.

It was late spring in 1990 that we first met with Frank at his home on Barnet Street in Roswell. The walls of his living room, as well as family room, were covered by his original landscape paintings. Each one of them had a story, but there was one in particular that left us with a haunting

Frank Kaufmann, seen here in 2000 shortly before his death, made a confession to the authors. Was he a hoaxer, a purveyor of disinformation, or a truth-teller?

image. Compared to other first impressions, Frank was rather reluctant to speak out on anything related to the 1947 affair. In fact, he spoke entirely as a secondhand observer. His account was strictly based on what he had heard at the time of specific events. In fact, as we advanced our investigation into the information he provided, he continuously asked us to keep his name out of it. As we started to pen our first book, *UFO Crash at Roswell*[2], he suggested that we not use his name. We assured him that he would only be portrayed as a secondhand source. And that was exactly the case.

Whether he was testing the waters or eventually accepted that he had a viable audience in our specific inquiry, Frank was about to move into phase two of his Roswell involvement. Beginning in 1991, Frank would claim that he was not only a player but that he was one of a select group of intelligence officers assigned to take charge of the entire recovery operation. "The Nine," as he maintained, immediately took control of the crash-retrieval operation under the command of the mysterious Robert Thomas from Washington, DC.[3] The more details Frank volunteered, the more we peppered him with enthusiastic questions. It appeared as though we finally had a first-hand witness who was not only privy to the most minute details of the crash but, more important than anything else, he slowly but surely claimed to see the bodies. He was opening up to only us, and he had drawings to back up his claims—artist that he was. That haunting painting hanging in his family room was making more sense to us.

Each and every time we met with Frank he presented himself more and more as the authority on the Roswell Incident. Along with his self-assuredness, he tantalized us with supportive documents, which at the time appeared to be in order. He displayed to us old sketches of an intact, damaged ship and its crew, all with one major caveat: Specific dates, locations, and descriptions were all contrary to what dozens of other witnesses had led us to believe. His pencil illustrations and descriptions of the craft and bodies were totally unlike what anyone else had visualized for us heretofore. The new testimony about the batwing-shaped "craft of unknown origin," as Frank loved to call it, brought a tinge of contemporary science fiction to the aging story. And his occupants of the fatally damaged ship looked serene—peaceful, even in death. In many ways it was as though he was trying to "humanize" the entire situation, and we soon considered him our "star" witness.[4] True, we would constantly wrestle with the concern that all the other witnesses couldn't be wrong. But Frank insisted that he saw it all, and if he was telling the truth, the others must be mistaken. He was in fact the very first of the former RAAF personnel who specified "Building 84" as the very hangar all the physical evidence transited through.[5] He would claim to have met both Charles Lindberg and Wernher von Braun in discussions about the crash.[6] Adding validity to his storyline were original "onion-skin" papers documenting his testimony. Additionally, throughout 1993 he began to sprinkle his story with more and more photographs, which he described as clandestine meetings with high-level officials where Roswell was the central ongoing theme. We still needed more, and he finally agreed to take us out to where it all happened. That fall, in what would be the first of many times, he rode along as he directed us to the sacred shrine of all Ufology: the Impact Site, where the ship and bodies were recovered. The gospel according to Frank Kaufmann was progressing in a linear direction, and, as he assumed the main role as the "Roswell Whistleblower," it was a story destined for Hollywood.

All during that time we were working on two deadline projects, one being our next book and the other finalizing the script for the *ROSWELL* movie, which was about to go into production. And just as before, with the first book, Frank requested his anonymity: He would not allow us to use his name in the follow-up book and refused to be portrayed in any form in the motion picture. Still, he remained entirely curious about both and would constantly call if he didn't hear from us as to new witnesses and what were they telling us. That in itself was starting to make us suspect motive in our relationship, but then Frank threw us for another loop. We were approached by producers at CBS, who expressed their desire to do a segment on Roswell for their highly rated news program *48 Hours*.[7] Given Frank's closet history, we never even asked him to be part of our witness pool. When the time came to conduct the principal filming in Roswell, CBS senior newsman Phil Jones took us aside and confided his personal opinion. "You know you have a very big story here. But I need something more, somebody more. Who is your best witness?" he asked.[8] We promised to contact "Frank" but with no guarantees. He must have been ready, as he shocked us all by agreeing to go on camera—but under strict conditions.

Frank Kaufmann inside Hangar P-3 (known today as Building 84), pointing out to the authors where the 1947 crash wreckage was strewn on the floor of the hangar. Photo from 1998.

Nonetheless, we were elated, so Frank and Phil Jones had dinner the next evening. The next day, we were all heading out to the impact site to shoot the interview with Frank. He would paint his verbal landscape on camera, but strictly over his shoulder. No one would see his face on network TV, but in many ways we felt he had come through for us, and he did not disappoint. During one take, Jones asked Frank, "How did you know that the bodies were not human?" Frank's unscripted reaction was priceless: "They sure weren't from Texas" he quipped. We all loved it. When the program finally aired in April 1994, Dan Rather ended the segment with the following pronouncement: "Truly something extraordinary crashed outside of Roswell, New Mexico, in July of 1947."[9] We now had CBS on our side and with no small thanks to Frank. But soon even greater scrutiny was about to develop.[10]

On numerous occasions, retired Colonel Arthur Jeffrey accompanied his commercial pilot son, Kent, to rendezvous with us in Roswell. Frank immediately hit it off with the officer, and they became good friends. It was after the CBS broadcast that Kent sponsored the prospect of a high-profile law firm being retained to represent the witnesses in a class-action suit against the U.S. government. Frank agreed to meet with attorney Edward G. Modell, of the renowned Dickstein, Shapiro & Morin Law Firm of Washington, DC. Modell and his assistant met behind closed doors with Frank for more than two hours and were permitted to question him in the same manner as they would vet a potential witness. The highly experienced criminal lawyer informed us later that he "couldn't shake Frank," and that he would be a "tough witness" in any courtroom.[11] Still, Frank was now telling us that the Mack Brazel debris field was "salted" with phony wreckage parts to divert attention away from the impact site. To further entice us, he showed us a piece of pumice stone, which he claimed was part of the ship. The claim eventually evolved into the stone being some of the crystallized ground from the impact site. Either way, we wanted the sample tested, at which Frank balked that he would never see it again. We remained far from convinced and always upped the ante. We started to demand the opportunity to speak with any of the two surviving members of "The Nine," one of whom was Robert Thomas, or whoever he really was. Frank started to lose favor with us as excuse after excuse wore thinner and thinner. There had to be someone who could verify his fantastic story. Would Frank help us to help himself? Not even his old friend Walter Haut would step forward and support his conflicting account of the events at Roswell. Walter disassociated himself totally from his now-former friend and became publicly critical of his testimony. It was for that reason that Walter Haut, one of the founders of the International Museum and Research Center in Roswell, never invited Frank to be part of the historic commemoration of the Incident. As far as Walter was concerned, Frank was not welcome through the front door.[12] We found ourselves using Frank's story as leverage against Walter's refusal to tell his entire story. We proceeded to chip away—at both of them.

At the time of the public viewing of the controversial *Alien Autopsy Film* in 1995 Frank stood his ground and publicly stated the body in the footage did not resemble the bodies recovered at Roswell in any way. We also immediately demanded that the promoters not associate their "video" with Roswell. As far as we were concerned, the further we could distance ourselves from that hoax, the greater likelihood that Frank would spell out more details to solidify his own position. Rather, it appeared to us that he was resting on his laurels and started to enjoy the spotlight. His face was becoming a regular on talk shows and in UFO documentaries. No more over-the-shoulder interviews.

Meanwhile, our search for additional witnesses continued unabated, and there remained one major obstacle in establishing the validity of one Frank J. Kaufmann: No other witnesses endorsed the case's most crucial details as he recounted them. Whereas Frank was the central figure in the book, *The Truth About the UFO Crash at Roswell* (1994), under the pseudonym of "Steve MacKenzie," we made every effort to investigate his claims, and by 1996 we began to have serious reservations about his veracity. For the first time thoughts of Frank playing the role of spoiler assigned to divert us from the truth crossed our minds. That same year, co-author Don Schmitt was scripting and producing the CD, *UFO Crash at Roswell: The Audio Documentary.* The production included more than 40 recorded Roswell witnesses describing their personal involvement, but Frank should have been the star witness. Demonstrative of the growing doubt, none of the abundant audio tracks of Frank were included. This was strictly Don Schmitt's decision and it became a harbinger of things to come.[13]

Another test of the truthfulness of a witness is when he or she is willing to put their names behind their stories. Numerous times we had urged Frank to put it down on paper, and each time he sheepishly declined. So when a witness we had never heard of before, retired Colonel Philip J. Corso, came out with the *New York Times* best-selling book, *The Day After Roswell,* which was timed for release at the time of the 50th anniversary, in July 1997, we looked at it as an opportunity lost. Frank had a much more engrossing account, but then we would later learn how involved he was with Corso. We watched with amusement at the celebration in Roswell at how Corso and Frank seemed to be long-lost friends. Our witness always shied away from the previous commemorations each July, but there he was sharing the limelight with Corso.[14] Amazingly, with more than 300 members of the press in town that weekend, Frank masterfully managed to elude them. Could we be wrong about our own "star witness"? Still, the star was about to go out.

Throughout the previous years, Frank often flaunted a letter postmarked from Washington, but with no return address—in fact, with no address at all. Taped to the outside was nothing more than a newspaper photograph of a much younger Frank. He insisted that officials at the post office knew exactly where it was to be sent.

Inside was a piece of paper cut in the shape of a trapezoid. Printed on it was a coded message intended solely for Frank supposedly instructing him to continue the ongoing secrecy pertaining to the events of 1947. Part of the cryptic message was the serial number "327A." Now, Frank was raised Roman Catholic, and many times spoke of his Catholic upbringing. His wife, Juanita, was Methodist. When we did a Google search on 327A it came up with only one connection: It was from a Methodist hymnal dating back to the '40s. To us, this was more than coincidence as we stared at the title of hymn 327A: "Thou Whilst Commest From Above."[15] We were flabbergasted with the knowledge that when Frank got married, he converted to Methodism. It was fall 1998 the next time Frank picked up the tab for breakfast at the Roswell Inn, and we threw an unexpected question at him. "Frank, tell us about that old Methodist hymn "Thou Whilst Commest From Above." Thank God there was a wall directly behind him as he immediately tipped back in his chair. Regaining his composure, he leaned forward toward us, smiled, and said, "Damn, you guys are good." That was all he would comment, but he gave us one of the widest smiles, which smacked of both approval and relief.

By that time, we had long discounted the impact site he had shown us and knew the correct one to be at another location. It became an ongoing joke between us and Frank whenever we visited his location. We would express our doubt, to which he would always gesture by crossing his arms and pointing in both directions. Frank was a smooth politician who was more at home with the Chamber of Commerce than the Army. We constantly observed that he lacked the hard military jargon one would expect from someone who was part of an elite intelligence unit assigned to recover a flying saucer. It continued to fall apart. And still Frank would promise to finally take us out to the real site and always brushed aside our increasing skepticism with "When it comes to nut-cracking time...."[16]

Hope waxing thinner and thinner, Frank threw another obstacle into the Roswell mix: He would provide us with the final proof, provided that "Edwards" would give him the okay—but not until then. According to Frank, Captain Edwards was his current liaison with his higher authorities and would occasionally check in with Frank to get a status report. Supposedly we were often the topic of conversation, and Frank would emphasize our persistence at getting to the truth. Each time Frank would inform us about another contact, he would assure us that it was just a matter of time.[17]

The Franklin Mint contracted with Frank to create a beautiful display of his Roswell ship.[18] Testor's model released two different kits, one of just the ship and the other a diorama of the impact site. Numerous sculptors and artists worked with Frank in re-creating displays of the ship, and finally Shadowbox produced the Roswell alien as depicted by Frank.[19] The Roswell commercial train continued at full steam, and Frank was the engineer. In today's contemporary world of public relations and controlling the narrative on any issue, Frank was totally compliant in promoting himself and his images of what happened in 1947. As Frank grew to accept that his time was running out, he asked Don Schmitt to take one of his three artist replicas of his bat-wing Roswell ship—"strictly on loan," but with the request that he use it as a visual display at future lectures. Schmitt respectfully declined.[20]

In the latter part of 1999, Frank was diagnosed with terminal bone cancer and given about a year to survive. After an initial stay at the Eastern New Mexico Medical Center, Frank was sent home to live out the rest of his time with family. Frank and Juanita had two children: a son and daughter who preceded them in death. It was their grandson Rick who arrived in Roswell to tend to his dying grandfather. In earnest, we made plans to secure Frank's last statements on the one thing that preoccupied us over the prior 10 years. Frank wanted to see Don Schmitt as soon as he was feeling stronger after the initial radiation treatments. Plans were set for mid-December.

An emaciated and weak Frank sat in his recliner in the family room. He leaned toward Schmitt, who was sitting on the sofa within a few feet of Frank. "Don, the game continues. The game continues," Frank exclaimed, as though still following the script. He would go even further by suggesting that someone new was "watching things." He apologized that he had no idea. He would humbly lament about the total indignity of dying of cancer and he was about as vulnerable as any human being could be at that time. It can be stated without doubt that Frank did not back away from most everything he ever stated about the Roswell Incident. He confirmed that there was a survivor from the crash, which he would never concede before. And he confessed that he had indeed taken us to a bogus crash site. If his condition permitted, he promised to show us the true site. Schmitt would make three more visits over the course of the next year.

During the next meeting, Frank's grandson Rick shocked all of us with a totally impromptu comment: "Tell Don about that piece of metal you brought home from the base." He casually went on to describe how his own father affirmed that he witnessed Frank take a piece of metal and pound it into a small cube with a hammer before releasing his grip, and it unraveled and smoothed out right before them.[21] At that point Juanita, standing next to her spouse's chair, exclaimed, "Yes, and I saw him do the same thing." Frank quickly reached over and dug his fingernails into her knee, giving her a most obvious message. Frank refused to say anything more about the topic and asked for additional pain medication.

"Have you heard anything from your Captain Edwards?" Schmitt asked. It was Rick who replied, "Some Air Force officer had called a number of times asking his [Frank's] condition." Rick informed Schmitt that the calls were from Texas and, while Frank was out of the room, gave him the return phone number.[22] "We need to still try to get your grandfather north of town," instructed Schmitt. All Rick could promise was to let us know when he improved enough, if at all, to make a long drive out into the desert. Chances were dwindling down rapidly as Frank's condition degraded.

As the clock was ticking down, we next focused on all of Frank's files. Regretfully for us, it was his final wish that all of his papers and other effects be willed to his three grandsons and granddaughter. "What about the museum?" Schmitt gently asked. "Can you get Walter [Haut] to come see me one last time?" Frank soberly requested. With the assistance of Walter's daughter, Julie Shuster, Frank had one of his dying wishes fulfilled. While they privately chatted in the family room, Julie was able to partially overhear their discussion from the adjoining front room. "They spoke for the first time in almost 10 years. Padre [Walter] didn't have much to say beyond Frank's condition. Whereas Frank spoke strictly about 1947 and hoped that his old friend would understand something," Julie reported.[23] On the drive back home, Walter didn't say a word.

We had arranged for our friend in Roswell, photographer Jack Rodden, to be on standby when Frank possibly had a good day. Frank had been a longtime friend of Rodden's dad, Ray. Jack pulled up his van in front of the house to assist Frank inside and then make the two-hour drive out to the correct crash location. He had been dressed for the occasion, and Rick would accompany him as well. Just as they were helping Frank into the vehicle, his frail bodily functions failed him, and us. It was never to happen.[24]

Over the next few weeks Frank became totally bedridden and was confined to his bedroom. Schmitt sat with him one last time, and they spoke of art and painting. It was time to say goodbye. But someone else was still keeping an eye on the situation.

Both Rick and Juanita were witness to the following scenario. Within a couple of weeks of the end, a chauffeured car pulled up in front of the residence. The driver opened the door for a military officer, who walked to the front door—and walked right in without so much as a knock. He proceeded to walk through the house and down the hallway. Frank's bedroom was down at the end on the right, and the Air Force officer knew where he was. The officer closed the door behind them. About a half hour passed before the intruder exited Frank's room and came back toward the family room. But instead of departing, he sat down in Frank's recliner, not uttering a word. After a few moments, assured that his mission was accomplished, he rose from the chair, turned to the front door, and let himself out. As though he were following strict military protocol, he never said a word to either civilian. Frank would only acknowledge that he stopped by to pay his respects.[25] Captain Edwards made sure the final chapter was closed. Frank J. Kaufmann quietly passed away on February 7, 2001. After the funeral services, Rick returned home to Seattle and 91-year-old Juanita was all alone for the first time in more than 55 years.

Both Jack Rodden and Julie Shuster stayed in frequent contact with Juanita, as did Don Schmitt. Each time the authors were in town, they would take her out to South Park Cemetery to see Frank. The first time they made such a visit, Juanita cried as she placed her hand on the headstone, "Why did you leave me with all this?" We made sure Frank's leased car was returned to the auto dealership and found a neighbor who would also check in with her each day, especially after Juanita swore that someone was in the house on one occasion. We agreed with the Roswell Police that she simply allowed her nighttime fears get the better of her. She always insisted there was a prowler.[26]

As long as Frank's files remained in the house, we still had high hopes of finding a possible smoking gun—maybe that piece of metal, which even Juanita confirmed to us after his death. She maintained that the military came to their home and retrieved it shortly after the

UFO incident. She added that Frank "got in a lot of trouble for walking off the base"with it.[27] She also confessed to us that Frank had driven her out to the crash site months after the cleanup. She had no idea how to return to the location after 50-some years. Frank had always promised that he had proof if it ever came to "nut-cracking time." If the story about the visit from the Air Force officer was true, we accepted that he wouldn't have left if he wasn't sure no proof contrary to the official position on Roswell remained. The allure was all the more compelling, as the jury was still out as to the credibility of Frank. We hoped his files would have the final answer.

After enough months had passed, Don Schmitt arranged for Center for UFO Studies scientific director Dr. Mark Rodeghier and colleague Mark Chesney to accompany him for a visit with Juanita. It was the first time she met these two gentlemen, and it would be the first time that she allowed anyone into Frank's office. While the other two researchers engaged in conversation with Frank's widow, Schmitt reached inside a desk after one of the upper side drawers had been removed. To his surprise there waiting, within his grasp, was a cardboard sachel. Without alerting Frank's widow to the developing situation, we indeed had found the smoking gun. Opening the sachel, there in plain sight were all the original documents that spelled out precisely who Frank Kaufmann truly was. Aside from these genuine papers, there were two vintage Underwood typewriters from the 1940s. There was a copy machine with the last attempts of cut-and-paste. There was an ample supply of blank, onion-skin paper—and Frank was an artist. Schmitt knew that Frank had a drawing table within his office and before Frank died asked to see his last work. Schmitt even suggested that Frank make some final drawings pertaining to 1947—any way to get both of them into his office. As it stood at that moment, it was fortunate he never was well enough to destroy all the evidence against him.

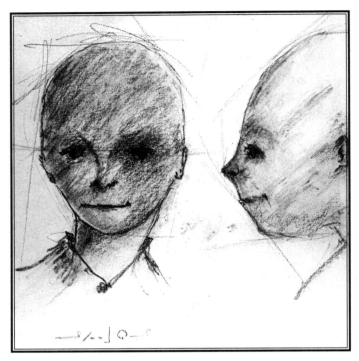

Original illustration of the bodies Kaufmann claimed to have seen at the crash site.

Due to our persistence, we discovered that all the documents pertaining to Roswell that Frank had long teased us with were forgeries. His separation record from the Army was a complete cut-and-paste alteration, and the papers that made any mention of "The Nine" were evidently typed by Frank. All of the photographs depicting Frank with high-ranking military officers and political dignitaries from Washington clearly recorded activities while he was with the Roswell Chamber of Commerce. They had nothing to do with events concerning 1947. A star witness had just been officially extinguished. We all agreed that nothing would be publicly disclosed until after Juanita was gone; she clearly had nothing to do with any deception on the part of her husband.[28]

Each member of the surviving family was questioned, and none of them were instructed by anyone to clear out Frank's office. Even when his cancer was first discovered, Frank still had more than a year to clear out all of the incriminating evidence against him. He also knew us well enough to know that we just wouldn't walk away once he was gone. Frank, who also was a regular member of the Roswell Masonic Temple, surely had some other confidant who could have beaten us to the treasure, yet he left it all. Was it for us?

Soon thereafter, we would also learn that Philip Corso had visited with Frank on two occasions to discuss 1947 while his own book was being written.[29] The obvious giveaway was that the Corso account of the immediate events surrounding Roswell in the opening pages of his tome are 100 percent Frank Kaufmann.

It was shortly after the *CBS 48 Hours* interview that we suggested Frank meet with President Bill Clinton. If the commander-in-chief was truly seeking the answers to Roswell, as he claims even to this day, Frank would not disappoint. We should have been surprised when Frank, without reservation, happily agreed, good Democrat that he was. Unfortunately, it was the president who showed no curiosity, and we know that the invitation did cross his very desk. Frank was also perfectly aware beforehand that we had contacts all the way to the Oval Office and still he said yes to our high-end proposal.[30]

In July 1995, when the then General Accounting Office (GAO) issued its *Results of a Search for Records Concerning the 1947 Crash Near Roswell, New Mexico* at the request of New Mexico Congressman Steven H. Schiff, little did we expect that the report would corroborate Frank. Four years previous to this incredible admission on the part of the U.S. federal government, Frank was stating to us that Roswell had "no paper trail"—that all the files had either been destroyed or were so cryptically encoded that "no one would ever find them."[31] As Schiff stated in his official press release, "The GAO report states that the outgoing messages from Roswell Army Air Field (RAAF) for this period of time were destroyed without proper authority." On one occasion, months before this announcement, Frank warned us, "There's nothing left to find."[32] Lucky prediction, or did he somehow know?

Another aspect of Frank's life that still bothers us is why someone, from "back east" no less, who had resided in Roswell for just two years up until that time, was shockingly entrusted to sit on the chamber of commerce. When we conducted a records search with the Roswell City Hall and acquired a copy of the very meeting minutes of the first time in which Frank was introduced to the rest of the chamber, it states, "Unlike all the other members of this group, Mr. Kaufmann will be paid by an *outside source*"[33] [authors' emphasis].

Who was Captain Edwards, and was that his real name? The phone number that Frank's grandson Rick provided was traced to a vacant office building in Houston, Texas. Was he the uninvited visitor just before Frank's death? And why didn't he show any concern about all the discrediting material in his home office?

Roswell pioneering researcher Stanton Friedman, who had always been both skeptical and critical of Frank, had been vindicated and was soon thereafter privately briefed on the situation. He remained a gentleman and honored our request of confidentiality until Juanita's passing.[34] The haunting painting that hung in Frank's family room had the face of one of his Roswell aliens painted in the background. He claimed that it was to preserve the memory of what he had seen in 1947.[35] The question remains: Did Frank ever witness anything out of the ordinary or did he merely get caught with his fingers in the cookie jar? Anyone who knew Frank would agree that he was capable of slipping classified evidence off the base. Upon his apprehension, was his punishment to remain in Roswell and mind the store? If anyone should ever come to Roswell and start snooping around, you just can't kick them out of town. That would raise even more questions. But you can divert, and you can put out a false story-line with the intent of taking them off the right path. And for years, that is precisely what Frank Kaufmann did—whether of his own volition or following orders from those individuals who still make it their business to cover up the true nature of Roswell. As Frank himself put it at the time his clock was running out, "The game continues."[36] The problem was that we played along for far too long, but we also were the ones who proved that their game was fixed—whether by Frank or someone else. We intend to find out.

CHAPTER 14

The Disappearance of Vernon Brazel: The True Story

From all the press accounts pertaining to any involvement of the Brazel family, the only mention of Mack's son Vernon is in the newspaper. The July 9, 1947, edition of the *Roswell Daily Record* ran the story with the headline "Harassed Rancher who Located 'Saucer; Sorry He Told About It." The article states how "Brazel related that on June 14 he and an 8-year old son, Vernon, were about 7 or 8 miles from the ranch house or the J.B. Foster ranch, which he operates, when they came upon a large area of bright wreckage made up on rubber strips, tinfoil, a rather tough paper and sticks."[1] The account went on to describe how "...on July 4 he, his wife, Vernon and a daughter Betty [sic], age 14, went back to the spot and gathered up quite a bit of the debris."

Aside from Mack and Vernon's age and the name of the owner of the ranch (J.B. Foster), the balance of the piece is entirely scripted for effect. Keep in mind that Brazel was in military custody at the time and was observed by no less than six individuals who witnessed the rancher being escorted by armed military officials to numerous media outlets in Roswell, most notably the *Roswell Daily Record*. For example, Brazel owned a home an hour and a half south of Roswell in Tularosa, New Mexico, where his family normally resided. There, they had running water, electricity, and daily contact with the outside world, whereas the ranch house on the Foster spread had no running water, no electricity, and was totally isolated from the rest of the world. Floyd and Loretta Proctor, their nearest neighbors, lived 10 miles away. The point is: Mack's wife, Maggie, and daughter, Bessie (her actual name), were not there at the time of the entire 1947 incident. As has been fully demonstrated over the past 25 years, it was the Proctor's son Dee who was with Mack when he discovered the debris field, not Vernon. And Vernon, who was at the ranch during that crucial time, secured a much more important role in this entire scenario—one that would generate a mystery we are just beginning to understand some 50 years later.

For the next 10 years of the youngest Brazel son's life, Vernon carried a family scourge he found hard to cope with. Back in Tularosa where he attended elementary school, he was the target of regular bullying. After all, his dad created a lot of fuss over a simple weather balloon, fool that he was. His son, therefore, had to be a fool as well. According to Loretta Proctor, "Vernon had adjustment problems. Kids who didn't know any better, always made fun of Vernon because of what Mack discovered."[2] True, many of the parents either saw enough or knew Mack well enough to know otherwise. Their children were shielded from the truth, but unfortunately poor Vernon was not provided such protection. Worst of all, he had to witness the utter humiliation and emotional stress exerted on his father.[3] Other boys could go to their dads for help. After his military detainment and the extent of both physical and mental abuse he was subjected to, Mack couldn't even help himself. The military made sure that they had him neatly wrapped up in a ball of sworn secrecy—including his family.

Still, there remained children who retained a special bond with Vernon. They shared a mutual experience they would be forced to never speak of again. The young Brazel was especially close to Dee Proctor. Not only were they about the same age, but his mother liked to call them the "little ranchers." They both helped Mack with chores and often rode with him across the open range.[4] There were other "little ranchers" that day when Mack found "something else," boys with the last names of Edington and Wright. And their lives would never be the same. Unable to talk with one another placed an additional strain on their friendships. They were forced to grow up overnight and literally had their childhoods stolen from them. Sadly, the difference with Vernon was that unlike all the others' fathers, his was at the very heart of what tormented them all. The son had clearly inherited the "sins of the father."

After graduating from Tularosa High School and having reached the legal age for enlistment into the military, Vernon joined the U.S. Navy. After completing his training in boot camp, he was commissioned as an enlisted sailor to the USS *Hassayampa*, which at that time was assigned to the Naval Dock at Pearl Harbor. First commissioned in April 1955 the *Hassayampa* was one of the most decorated fleet oilers in the entire Navy's replenishment group. During Vernon's tenure, the ship was deployed numerous times in the West Pacific to assist the 7th Fleet.[5] Curious that a young man born and reared in New Mexico, in the heart of the desert, would be drawn to the Navy—but then again the Brazels had a falling out with the Army back in '47, and the wounds would never heal.

Depending on what side of the fence one was on, the name Brazel became synonymous with either the term *flying saucer* or *balloon fiasco*, and Vernon couldn't escape either. The Navy couldn't take him far enough away, and upon returning home, he seldom if ever spoke of any high sea adventures or naval exploits. It was as though he just moved out of the area for two years and came home to wash his clothes. Still, the Brazel family saw him as a "young sailor coming home who had his whole life ahead of him."[6] But the fates had other plans for Vernon Brazel.

Over the course of the next year, Vernon found himself in Virginia, then California, and then returned to New Mexico. He took a job working for a ranch in Grants and appeared to have finally settled down to some state of normalcy. He had a small house and a car, and like most virale young men started a relationship with a young lady. Maybe time had healed old scars and the time for looking forward was about to take at least one of the Brazels into the Promised Land. But then word came that provided Vernon with another opportunity to run. His parents, Mack and Maggie, had decided to move to Alaska—alone. Vernon pleaded to join them, to try for another start, but finances were tight and their son was rejected—again. To Vernon, Dad was once again turning his back. It was 1947 all over again, and Vernon was beyond angry. He seriously considered rejecting them in return. But let it be stated for the record: Vernon's animosity was directed strictly at his parents. No other members of the Brazel family were involved.[7]

Has anyone seen Vernon? Concerned calls circulated throughout Grants and eventually to the rest of his relations in Capitan, New Mexico. His mother and father were out of reach in Alaska for the time being—and why worry them? One member of the family went so far as to suggest that he hitched a ride with some trucker and was on his way to Fairbanks, Alaska, where his parents had recently moved, at that very moment. But as the days passed and the state police in Grants were called in to investigate a missing person report, matters became disconcerting. First, his abandoned car was found just outside the city with no indication of foul play or clues as to what became of him. Next, the situation became more worrisome as his lady friend was questioned and, like all the others, hadn't seen or heard from Vernon in days—without so much as a goodbye. And what clearly suggested some underhanded dilemma involving the 21-year-old Brazel was that his last paycheck went unclaimed. No money was drawn from his checking account, and his house wasn't listed for sale. Vernon had disappeared, and it was up to the police to find him, no matter what the outcome. Mack and Maggie were contacted in Alaska. No truck arrived with any passenger named Brazel.

As the days, then weeks and hopeless months passed, no answers were forthcoming. In fact, the state police assigned to investigate the disappearance were less than cooperative. And if one didn't know better, they started to behave as if they had something to hide. Vernon's brother-in-law, James Schreiber, made repeated inquiries to law enforcement at the state level and was constantly told to "stay out of it."[8] The family feared the worst and eventually resigned themselves to accept that Vernon was not coming back. No one—not a single member of the Brazel family or anyone else who personally knew Vernon Brazel—would ever hear from him again. No human remains were ever discovered, no ransom notes, not a single shred of evidence that would shine any light on such an abrupt disappearance. Another key witness to the events of 1947 had met an untimely demise, and this time, the survivors were not even granted any closure, which made his loss all the more hurtful—and intimidating. Which of the Brazels would be next?

During the frantic search for their son, Mack and Maggie had moved back to New Mexico. Within three years, on October 1, 1963, Mack suffered a fatal heart attack at the young age of 64. His own father, William Ware Brazel, had lived to 81. A year later, Vernon's nephew, William R. Brazel, was shot to death while rifle hunting with two companions. One of the other hunters was mortally wounded from a second shot; the state police in Grants concluded both shots were accidental. To this day the family maintains that the deaths were not coincidental.[9] Years later, when a records search request was made through that same state police office as to the final case file report on Vernon, the state capital office in Santa Fe archived the report, which stated that the young Brazel had accidentally "drowned while fishing."[10] First, the state law officials tell the Brazels to stay out of it and then withhold the results of their investigation. Why?

Most families would have perceived more than a subtle message in such an ongoing tragedy. Some might argue that with even the most subtle overtone of outside instigation with the Brazel affairs, such manipulators would have faced the wrath of the offended. As Vernon's older brother, Bill, would remark, "If anyone had any thoughts of threatening the Brazels, we would have called out the clan."[11] But when we pushed him further as to whom he suspected might be responsible, he had to concede, "These were shadows. How do you fight shadows?" As a result, the Brazels retreated, and for the next 25 years the family concentrated on ranching. Memories of 1947 seldom came up, though occasionally someone would make a passing remark about the true fate of Vernon. Cattle and sheep needed to be tended and displayed no emotion for the living.

The year was 1978 when researchers Len Stringfield and Stan Friedman spoke to an aging intelligence officer who described to them holding pieces of a flying saucer. Jesse Marcel reopened the Roswell Incident after 30 years of silence. Soon the Brazels would be drawn into that moment of history they had tried so hard to forget. Friedman's investigative partner, William L. Moore, interviewed Mack's older sister Lorraine Ferguson, Bill, wife Shirley, and sister Bessie for their forthcoming book *The Roswell Incident*.[12] Personal details were not discussed, and the disappearance of Vernon was only stated as a matter of fact with no resolution. The Brazels remained an extremely private family and had been warned in the past about speaking out of turn. Aside from Vernon's niece Fawn going on camera in 2006, the only other time that a member of the Brazel family went on film during that time was the HBO interview of Bill, for the 1985 documentary *UFOs—What's Going On?* Brazel focused entirely on the "scraps" of material that he had examined from the crash. Vernon was never mentioned in either recorded interview.[13] He had vanished back in 1960, and that's all any of the Brazel family knew. That was, until 2002.

It was during that May that a strange phone call came from an unknown woman by the name of Jean Tanniehill.[14] She was calling from Helena, Montana. "My late husband was named Edward Tanniehill but I'm looking for anyone who can give me information on Vernon Brazel." The woman mispronounced the last name as the South American country. The unexpected call was received by Bessie Schreiber's son Brazel in Portland, Oregon—because of his name. Jean's daughters, Sherry and Fawn, had Googled the name—the name that came up when Jean had applied for Social Security, and her late husband's own number came up with another name: Vernon Brazel. The only information that Vernon's nephew could provide was that he had disappeared some 40 years before, and not a word was heard from him since. Jean explained that she not only had possible new information but wanted to know the whereabouts of Vernon's immediate family. Her next search for answers would take her to Capitan, New Mexico—but would anyone believe her?

Bessie Brazel Schreiber (seated), daughter of Mack Brazel, gave the authors Tom Carey (L) and Don Schmitt (R) her last interview about the 1947 events. Photo from 1999.

Bill received an immediate call from his then-estranged sister, Bessie. He laughed it off, but nevertheless the news caught his attention. The more he considered it, the more curious he became. No matter, he was still pleased to once again talk with Bessie. Jean's daughters would e-mail photographs of their father to Bessie, who next forwarded them on to Bill's son Joe. Like Bessie, Bill knew he was staring his brother in the eye as he would have appeared in the immediate years after he was last seen. The longer he focused on the photos, the more remorseful he became and, after all the wasted years of not talking with Bessie, he wasn't about to repeat that same hurt. She agreed that it was time to reconcile and visit with her older brother, hopefully with good news about their long-lost brother. It would be the last time they would see one another.[15]

Edward Tanniehill's widow arrived in Capitan too late. Bill had quietly passed away just weeks before, on April 2, 2003. He died with the confidence that his brother had lived to see more days beyond the time he was snatched from their lives. Bill died with the answers to questions for which they had lost hope many years before. He was at peace with the news. Now it was Jean with all the questions. Who was this man with two identities who would become her husband and was somehow connected to the story of a "flying saucer"? But before traveling down to Capitan, she went to where it all began: Corona.

Geraldine Perkins ran the general store in the little cattle town of Corona in 1947. She had one of the two phones in the entire region, and it was there that Mack Brazel made the urgent call to his boss J.B. Foster in Texas about the crash debris. Fifty-six years later, someone new arrived at her home asking questions about one of Mack's sons. Like everyone else, Perkins, then almost blind, stated to Jean Tanniehill that no one had ever seen or heard anything from Vernon for many years. Tanniehill next explained to her who she was and what had actually become of Vernon, and that she was on her way to meet with the Brazels in Capitan. No sooner than Jean's departure, Perkins's phone again lit up with talk about the Brazels.[16] The story she related was unbelievable—especially to neighbors like Loretta Proctor, who quickly surmised that it must have something to do with 1947. She said, "Back then, those boys saw something they weren't supposed to see and now Vernon will never talk."[17]

Imagine the same circumstances when you first discover that your husband isn't who he says he is, and then you meet with his actual family many years later. As awkward as it should have been, the surviving Brazel family welcomed Jean to the Bill Brazel ranch in Capitan. As puzzled and confused as everyone in Joe and Beverly Brazel's home was, there was an abundance of relief just to finally know the truth, as it was exchanged between both families.

The story of Vernon's missing years went like this: Vernon Brazel arrived in Helena, Montana, in 1960 with the new name of Edward Tanniehill. He met and married Jean shortly thereafter. He insisted that he had no family, relatives, or hometown. He had the name of "Vernon" tattooed on his arm; he claimed it was his long-passed father. He had no prior history that he confided to her, and he was a heavy drinker. They had two daughters named Sherry and Fawn, which just happened to be the names of Vernon's actual nieces. No cards, letters, or phone calls ever came from out of state for Jean's husband, and with the young girls, she was more concerned with their well-being and Edward's incessant binges. If he had a troublesome past, he never shared it, but he was clearly traumatized by something. The drinking got worse and started to affect his work at a car garage he owned and operated until, in 1967, just seven years after he left New Mexico, he would leave another family: He took a gun and killed himself. Sherry and Fawn were barely starting school and have little to no recollections of the father who decided to abandon them, but whether a result of the excessive liquor abuse or the mental anguish that tormented him, it still caused his family a tremendous burden. Fortunately the girls were too young to absorb the pain. For Jean, it was partly a relief to see the end of all the torture from the demons in her husband's mind—not to mention the hurt to move forward and play both mother and father to the children. The Brazels listened and sat totally flabbergasted. Soon the shock turned into embarrassment at the awareness that Vernon had betrayed his family, not to mention what he did to theirs.[18]

Maybe in his youth Vernon truly did see something that he shouldn't have. Maybe he had nothing to say about his final disposition or his final fate. Ironic that Jesse Marcel, Jr., would arrive in Helena to live out the balance of his life just a few years after Vernon. Whether they could have known each other was one point of conjecture on the part of both families. Vernon was gone four years before Dr. Marcel initially walked into town in 1971. Nevertheless, the true story—for what little we know of the complete story—boggles the mind and has few, if any, comparisons. The actions of the New Mexico State Police were not only unprofessional but also suggested suppression of the facts. Under whose authority? The surviving members of the Brazel and Tanniehill families now have closure—but nonetheless are no closer to any resolution as to why someone just walks out on all of their loved ones and then takes on a new identity to ensure not ever being found. The IRS, bill collectors, and former spouses—none of these could account for the disappearance.

After more than 50 years, the final question remains, considering who the real Vernon Brazel was, and what he was supposed to have witnessed: Was he someone else's liability? And so, were steps taken to isolate him and place him in a form of protective custody, so he could never tell the world "his" true story and, in the process, never see his family and friends again? As with too many of the witnesses, including the children of Roswell, sadly, we will never know. And that remains the unfinished chapter in the Mack Brazel family book. As we and both families still ponder: If Vernon Brazel's/Edward Tanniehill's demons arrived in a flying saucer, neither man could escape them. And that remains the unfinished chapter in this book.

Chapter Notes

Introduction

1. First Lieutenant Walter Haut, Roswell Army Air Field, Public Information Officer, 1947.

2. *One of ours* is a long-standing term going back to World War II. Whenever American military observed approaching military hardware on the battlefield, hearing it was "one of ours" always resulted in a sigh of relief. This would certainly extend to the crash of a craft of unknown origin back in 1947.

3. Rosemary A. McManus, Personal interview, 1994.

4. *Roswell Daily Record*, July 9, 1947.

5. Radio station reporter Frank Joyce of KGFL, as told to him by Mack Brazel. In-person interviews with Joyce, 1998–2002.

6. Stated by Brigadier General Roger Ramey on an El Paso radio station a few days after his weather balloon press conference.

7. *Upstairs* is military jargon for the "higher-ups"—in other words, the senior officers who make all the decisions and are the only ones who have the need to know about all matters classified TOP SECRET.

8. Air Intelligence Requirements Division (AIRD), "Draft of Collection Memorandum," October 28, 1947. This document outlined the essential elements of information required to analyze flying disk reports effectively, which included the Roswell Incident.

Chapter 1

1. "Harassed Rancher Who Located 'Saucer' Sorry He Told About It," *Roswell Daily Record*, July 9, 1947.

2. Loretta Proctor, personal interviews, 1989–2010.

3. Truman Pierce, Bill Brazel, Loretta Proctor, and Juanita Sultemeier, personal interviews, 1990 and 1999.

4. Loretta Proctor, personal and telephone interviews, 1989–2010.

5. Sydney Jack Wright, personal interview, 1999.

6. Fawn Fritz, personal interviews, 2002–2015.

7. Dee Proctor, in-person meeting, circa 1989.

8. Quotes and information in this paragraph from Loretta Proctor, personal and telephone interviews, 1989–2010.

9. Robert Porter, personal interview, 1990. Aside from being Loretta Proctor's brother, Robert Porter was stationed at the RAAF in 1947 and was a crewman on the B-29 Bomber *Dave's Dream*, which transported Major Jesse Marcel and the first shipment of wreckage to Fort Worth Army Air Field in Texas, on July 8, 1947.

10. Quotes and information in this paragraph from Loretta Proctor, personal and telephone interviews, 1989–2010.

11. Mary Ann Strickland and Juanita Sultemeier, personal interviews, 1990.

12. Lerry Bond and Gary McDaniel, personal and telephone interviews, 1999, 2000. Both Deputy Bond and Judge McDaniel individually attempted numerous times to discuss the 1947 incident with Dee Proctor, failing at each opportunity. One might think that a civilian might be more inclined to "confess" a situation involving the authorities with an officer of the law and a judge sworn to uphold those laws. Dee was not impressed and behaved with them, as with us, by refusing to discuss the matter.

13. Loretta Proctor, personal interviews, 1989–2010.

14. Ibid.

15. Jeff Wells, personal interviews, 1989–1994. Wells, who was especially helpful in referring us to possible witnesses, described to us that as long as he was the ranch foreman, he was of the impression that there were two specific sites related to the 1947 incident. Wells also ensured that we maintain a present-day working relationship with the current owners of the ranch.

16. John Purdy, personal interviews, 1994–1995. Purdy is an award-winning British producer and director of *The Roswell Incident*, released by the BBC in 1995.

17. Kevin Randle, telephone interview with Timothy "Dee" Proctor, 1997.

18. Prince Hans Adam II, personal meeting in Washington, DC, 1990.

19. Dr. Richard Glaze, handwritten note, 1960.

Chapter 2

1. Randle, Kevin D., and Donald R. Schmitt, *The Truth About the UFO Crash at Roswell* (New York: Avon Books, 1994), p. 17.

2. Fawn Fritz, in-person interview, 2006; Ardeth Vandercook, telephone interview, 2000.

3. Quotations in this paragraph from Frank Joyce, in-person interviews, 1998-2002.

4. *Albuquerque Journal*, July 9, 1947; *San Antonio Express*, July 9, 1947; and *Houston Post*, July 9, 1947, per *www.roswellproof.com*.

5. Randle and Schmitt, *The Truth About the UFO Crash at Roswell*, p. 87.

6. See Chapter 9: "The Senator and the Aliens—'Get Me the Hell Out of Here!'" in *Witness to Roswell: Unmasking the Government's Biggest Cover-Up* (Franklin Lakes, N.J.: New Page Books, 2009), pp. 87–95.

7. Pete and Mary Anaya, in-person interviews, September 2002.

8. Jack Rodden, in-person interview, 1990.

9. Barbara Duggar, videotaped interview in *Recollections of Roswell II* (Mt. Rainier, Md.: Fund for UFO Research, Inc., 1992); also Barbara Duggar, telephone interviews, 2015.

10. Information and all quotations in this section from Sue Farnsworth Bennett, in-person and telephone interviews, 2008.

11. George Cisneros, telephone interviews, 2008.

12. Information and quotations in this section from Michelle Penn, telephone interview conducted by Anthony Bragalia, 2008.

13. Sue Farnsworth Bennett, in-person interviews, 2008.

14. Information and quotations in this section from Michelle Penn, telephone interview conducted by Anthony Bragalia, 2008.

15. Ibid.

16. Family of Patrick Saunders, in-person interviews, 1991 and 1995.

17. Information and quotations in this section from Michelle Penn, telephone interview conducted by Anthony Bragalia, 2008.

18. Carey and Schmitt, *Witness to Roswell: Unmasking the Government's Biggest Cover-Up.*

Chapter 3

1. The Wilcox's daughter, Phyllis (age 24 in 1947), was married to Ralph McGuire, who at the time was a pilot in the Air Corps. While he was away in service, Phyllis and their son were living with her parents, George and Inez, at the sheriff's residence located over the sheriff's office in the Roswell courthouse. The other Wilcox daughter, Elizabeth (age 23 in 1947), was married to a World War II veteran named Jay Tulk. They lived on a ranch in the Dexter-Hagerman area of New Mexico just southeast of Roswell, but they visited the courthouse residence often.

2. The only radio news broadcasts involving the Roswell UFO events from 1947 that survive to us today were those made by announcer Taylor Grant on the national *ABC Nightly News* of July 8 and 9, 1947.

3. The first poll regarding flying saucers was a Gallup Poll taken on August 14, 1947. It showed that most people responded that they did not know what they were, followed by atmospheric and celestial events, hoaxes, and secret U.S. programs. Russian devices only came in at 1 percent, and interplanetary spaceships did not make the list as a separate item but likely was among those in the 9 percent "other" category. The poll results are most easily accessible at *www.project1947.com/fig/gallup.htm*.

4. Quotations here from Frank Kaufmann, telephone interview, 2001.

5. Jack Rodden, personal interview, 1990.

6. "Sheriff Wilcox Takes Leading Role in Excitement Over Report 'Saucer' Found," *Roswell Daily Record*, July 9, 1947.

7. Brigadier General [one star] Roger M. Ramey was the commanding officer of the "Mighty" 8th Air Force headquartered in Fort Worth, Texas, at the time of the Roswell events of July 1947. The 509th Bomb Group in Roswell was under his command, and the "weather balloon" press conference was held in his office in Fort Worth on the afternoon of July 8, 1947, effectively killing the flying saucer crash story at that point. Ramey would later become the Air Force's "UFO Guy." He died in 1963, but not before admitting to his wife, LaTane, that the 1947 Roswell crash was that of a spaceship.

8. The 509th Bomb Group was created during World War II solely to drop the atomic bomb, and it was two of these delivered by 509th B-29s, *Enola Gay* and *Bockscar,* on Hiroshima and Nagasaki that ended the war. By 1947, the 509th had re-deployed to Roswell, New Mexico, with its atomic mission remaining intact

and rendering it the most elite unit in the U.S. arsenal at the time. The 509th Bomb Wing still exists today at Whiteman AFB in Missouri, where its nuclear mission remains the same. Only the aircraft have changed: from the WW II B-29 "Superfortress" bombers of 1947 to the B-2 "Spirit" stealth bombers of today.

9. Berlitz, Charles, and William L. Moore, *The Roswell Incident* (New York: Grosset & Dunlap, 1980).

10. Randle, Kevin D., and Donald R. Schmitt, *UFO Crash at Roswell* (New York: Avon Books, 1991).

11. Phyllis McGuire, *Recollections of Roswell Part II* (Mt. Rainier, Md.: Fund for UFO Research, Inc., 1992).

12. Randle and Schmitt, *UFO Crash at Roswell.*

13. McGuire, *Recollections of Roswell Part II.*

14. Barbara Duggar, telephone interview, March 2015.

15. Ibid.

16. Ibid. See also *Recollections of Roswell Part II.*

17. Ibid.

18. Randle and Schmitt, *The Truth About the UFO Crash at Roswell.* NOTE: The distance of the Impact Site from Roswell—30 miles north of town—was confirmed again in 2015 by Frankie Rowe, whose father, a Roswell City fireman, reached the site in his fire truck on July 7, 1947.

19. The body count (two dead and one still alive) at this site was confirmed by Frankie Rowe in 2015, based upon her father's account, who was a Roswell City fireman at the site in question on July 7, 1947.

20. Randle and Schmitt, *The Truth About the UFO Crash at Roswell.*

21. Ibid.

22. Phyllis McGuire, personal interview, January 1990.

23. Barbara Duggar, telephone interview, March 2015.

24. Barbara Duggar, *Recollections of Roswell Part II.*

25. Barbara Duggar, telephone interview, March 2015.

26. 26. Ibid.

27. Elizabeth Tulk, *Recollections of Roswell Part II*.

28. Barbara Duggar, telephone interview, March 2015.

29. Ibid (all in this paragraph, unless otherwise noted).

30. Phyllis McGuire, telephone interview, December 1989.

31. Barbara Duggar, telephone interview, March 2015.

32. Jay Tulk as originally told to Don Schmitt in 1992.

33. Barbara Duggar, telephone interview, March 2015.

34. Carey, Thomas J. & Donald R. Schmitt, *Witness to Roswell*, New Jersey: Pompton Plains, 2007, 2009.

35. Barbara Duggar, telephone interview conducted March, 2015.

36. Ibid.

37. Ibid.

38. All George McGuire quotes from a telephone interview conducted July 2015.

Chapter 4

1. Radio station WHDH Talk Radio 850AM, Boston, Massachusetts. Host Larry Glick, Awarded Massachusetts Broadcasting Hall of Fame.

2. Bill Brazel, personal interviews, 1989–2003.

3. Frankie Rowe, personal interviews, 1989–2015.

4. Dave Ford, investigation of Arthur Philbin in association with New York State Police, 1992. (The investigation of former NY State Police officer Arthur Philbin was conducted by Skip Tracer, "David Ford," of Kalamazoo, Michigan.)

5. Frankie Rowe, as told to her by her father, Dan Dwyer. Personal interviews with Frankie Rowe, 1989–2015.

6. Ibid.

7. Lee Reeves, phone interview with family, 2011.

8. C.C. Woodbury (son of C.M. Woodbury), personal interview, 2011.

9. Helen Cahill, personal interview, 1993.

10. Numerous business owners in Roswell in 1947, including Art McQuiddy, editor of *The Roswell Morning Dispatch,* and Judd Roberts, minority owner of radio station KGFL.

11. All from Ken Letcher, personal interviews, 2012 – 2015.

12. Frankie Rowe, personal interview, 1997.

13. Chester Lytle, personal interview, 1998. In his capacity as a designing engineer at Motorola in Chicago at the time of the Manhattan Project, Lytle was involved in the invention of the radio detonators of "Little Boy" and "Fat Man," the two atomic bombs dropped on Japan in 1945.

14. Frankie Rowe, personal interview, 1997.

15. Brian A. Philbin, telephone interview, 2012. Contrary to the speculative information passed onto Dave Ford from the New York State Police about the aftermath of Arthur Philbin, his son stated that his father was a devout Catholic, was not a heavy drinker, and moved to Nebraska after leaving the service. He did concur that his father, due to his large stature, booming voice, and formidable presence, was very intimidating. He added that he was a true patriot and that "God and country" came first while he served in the military.

Chapter 5

1. Carey and Schmitt, *Witness to Roswell.*

2. All here from interviews conducted by Jeff Peronto, England, 1990. Peronto was a college music director and videographer. Co-author Schmitt had arranged for Peronto to film the interviews while on a music project in the UK.

3. Carey and Schmitt, *Witness to Roswell.*

4. Peronto interviews. (See note #2 from this chapter.)

5. Ibid.

6. Ibid.

7. Sappho Henderson, personal interview, 1991.

8. All John Kromschroeder quotes from personal interview, 1990.

9. Both quotations in this paragraph from Sappho Henderson, personal interview, 1991.

10. Mary Katherine Groode, personal interview, 1991.

11. Recollection and quotations from John G. Tiffany, personal interview, 1990. Tiffany's father described their concern about contamination after the special flight to Wright Field. It could be suggested that their anxiety was due to fear of radiation given their aircraft was a B-29 Bomber designed to deploy atomic bombs. Given the very nonchalant attitude the military had for negative effects of radiation from 1945 through the time of the incident, Tiffany's fear was no doubt centered on the unusual cargo, and where it possibly originated.

12. Edwin Easley, Lieutenant Colonel USAFR, telephone interviews, 1990, 1991.

13. Nancy Strickland, Personal interviews, 1992, 1993, 2002, 2003.

14. Ibid.

15. All quotations and recollection from Mary Ann Gardner, telephone interviews, 1990, 1991.

16. Ibid.

17. We were looking for the "dying female archaeologist" who passed away in 1976 in the hospital in St. Petersburg, Florida, where Maryanne Gardner was a nurse who had cared for this person. She had claimed to have been with a group of archaeologists or geologists who had been out fossil-hunting that day when they came upon the downed alien craft and crew. She was very scared, according to Gardner, about telling Gardner the story. After a short while, she passed away, leaving

no friends or relatives, and Gardner could not recall her name. The hospital refused to permit author Don Schmitt to look through the hospital records for 1976 to try to get a name or two from the time period to give to Gardner to hopefully identify the woman.

Upon learning of that dead end, in 1992 author Tom Carey went to the University of Pennsylvania's Museum of Archeology and Anthropology and started going through the 1976 issues of various archeology periodicals and journals, hoping to find an obituary for a female archaeologist in or from Florida who fit the description given to us by Maryanne Gardner. He found one in the periodical *Current Anthropology* in one of its 1976 issues. Her name was Evelyn Kessler. But by that time Maryanne Gardner had stopped cooperating with us by not taking phone calls. Carey wrote her a letter with a number of female names listed, including that of Evelyn Kessler (sort of like a police lineup), and asked Gardner if any of the names listed rang a bell with her. Gardner never responded.

18. Carey and Schmitt, *Witness to Roswell*.

19. Edgar Skelley, Lieutenant Colonel USAFR, telephone interview, 1990.

20. Anne Skelley, in-person communication, 2002.

21. Ibid.

22. Robert Slusher, telephone discussion, 2002. We used similar tactics in providing potential witnesses an opportunity to speak with a former colleague. In 1994, when the then–Secretary of the Air Force, Sheila E. Widnall, absolved former Air Force personnel of their security oaths concerning Roswell, from that time on we demonstrated her statement to former military personnel. Time and time again, the retired servicemen reminded us that what happened in 1947 was an *Army* incident; the *Air Force* didn't even exist at that time.

23. Anne Skelly, telephone interview, 2002.

24. Anne Skelly, telephone call, 2010.

Chapter 6

1. Quotations and recollection to start the chapter from Carey and Schmitt, *Witness to Roswell.*

2. Marcel, Jr., Jesse, and Linda Marcel, *The Roswell Legacy: The Untold Story of the First Military Officer at the 1947 Crash Site* (Franklin Lakes, N.J.: The Career Press/New Page Books, 2009).

3. Ibid.

4. Tape-recorded telephone conversation between Jesse Marcel, Sr., and Jesse Marcel, Jr., 1979, provided to authors, 1990.

5. All quotes here from "Pete" Haut, personal interviews, 1989–1990.

6. Lloyd Thomson, telephone conversations, 1990.

7. Jesse Marcel, Jr., and Crash Conference, Washington, DC, May 1990. Don Schmitt was a participant and helped arrange the 11 witnesses.

8. Ibid.

9. Marcel and Marcel, *The Roswell Legacy.*

10. Brad Radcliffe served as Don Schmitt's research associate from 1989 to 1995. At the time he was counselor at the Milwaukee County Drug and Alcohol Administration Office. At Schmitt's request, Radcliffe secured the assistance of Dr. Watkins in order to hypnotically regress Dr. Marcel back to 1947.

11. NBC *TODAY* producer, who has requested anonymity, informed us that it was co-host Bryant Gumbel who refused to air any portion of the Watkins/Marcel hypnosis session.

12. Linda Marcel, personal interviews, 1997–2015. Family and close friends called Marcel "Jess."

13. All here from Jesse Marcel, Jr., personal telephone interviews, 1990-2013.

14. Denise Marcel, personal interviews, 2004–2015.

15. Jesse Marcel, Jr., personal telephone interviews 1990-2013.

16. Denise Marcel, personal interviews, 2004–2015.

Chapter 7

1. Rosemary A. McManus, personal interview, 1994

2. George H. Bush, personal interviews, 1990, 1991.

3. Roswell Historical Society records.

4. Glenn Dennis, personal interview, 1990.

5. George H. Bush, personal interviews, 1990, 1991.

6. George H. Bush and Jenny L. Overton, personal interview and telephone interviews, 1990, 2006.

7. Ibid.

8. George H. Bush, personal interviews, 1990, 1991.

9. Ibid.

10. Jenny L. Overton, personal interview and telephone interviews, 1990, 2006.

11. Ibid.

12. Patricia A. Bush, personal interviews, 2004–2006. The Bush family remains convinced that foul play was at hand in the bizarre circumstances surrounding Miriam's death. There was no investigation beyond the immediate discovery of her body, and no autopsy was performed to dispute the coroner's conclusion of suicide.

13. Jenny L. Overton, telephone conversation, 2007.

14. Victor Golubic, quoted in Pflock, *Roswell: Inconvenient Facts*.

Chapter 8

1. John Kromschroeder, videotaped interview in *Recollections of Roswell, Part II* (Mount Rainier, Md.: The Fund for UFO Research, 1992).

2. Randle and Schmitt, *UFO Crash at Roswell*.

3. John Kromschroeder, videotaped interview, 1992.

4. Carey and Schmitt, *Witness to Roswell*.

5. Lloyd Nelson, telephone interview, 2002. NOTE: PFC Lloyd Nelson clerked for 1st Lieutenant Walter Haut in the RAAF PIO Office in 1947.

6. Julie Shuster, in-person interviews conducted over many years. Julie is the late daughter of Walter Haut and the former director of the International UFO Museum & Research Center in Roswell, New Mexico.

7. Ibid.

8. Carey and Schmitt, *Witness to Roswell*.

9. Ibid.

10. Ibid.

11. Eugene Smith, Jr., telephone interview, 2005.

12. Ibid.

13. Thomas Gonzales, in-person interview, 2000.

14. Loretta Proctor, in-person interviews, 1989–90 and 1994–95.

15. Ibid.

16. The original and first-discovered Roswell UFO crash site is actually located 75 miles northwest of the city of Roswell and about 30 miles south–southeast of the small town of Corona, New Mexico. It contained most of ground-wreckage from the exploded alien craft and is known today as the Mack Brazel or Foster Ranch "Debris Field Site." Located 2 1/2 miles east of the Brazel Site is what we call the "Dee Proctor Body Site," which is where we believe two alien crew members fell to Earth to their demise after being expelled from their extraterrestrial craft when it exploded. The inner cabin or an escape pod within the craft was able to withstand the explosion and remained

aloft for an additional 35 miles in an east–southeast direction, coming to rest 40 miles north–northwest of the city of Roswell. That location is known as the final "Impact Site," where two deceased and one "live" alien were found.

17. Jack Rodden, in-person interview, 1990.

18. Ibid.

19. Leroy Lange, in-person interview, 1998.

20. Hope Balda, in-person interview, 1998.

21. Bill Brazel, in-person interview, 1989.

22. Ibid.

23. Ibid. NOTE: Readers will recall that Bill Brazel had stored some pieces of crash wreckage that he had found on the Foster ranch over the course of two years following the 1947 crash in a cigar box. Somehow the military found out about it and showed up at Brazel's home in 1949 demanding the cigar box, which Bill Brazel duly handed over to them.

24. Ibid.

25. L.D. Sparks, in-person interview, 2000. NOTE: Please see Tom Brookshier's comment in Chapter 12 regarding a piece of the crash wreckage he witnessed that seemed to "float in the air."

26. Ibid.

27. Trini Chavez, in-person interview, 2005.

28. Ibid.

29. Ibid.

30. Ibid.

Chapter 9

1. History of Timkin Company, Timkin Company Website. Founded 1899, Henry, H.H., & William Timken, Timken Roller Bearing Co.

2. See Chapter 12.

3. Personal interviews conducted by William E. Jones and Irena McCammon, *Ohio UFO Notebook*, 1994.

4. Ed Balint, *The Repository: Canton's Close Encounter,* August 22, 2010.

5. Roswell City Directory, 1947.

6. James Wood, telephone interview, 2012.

7. Frank Vega, personal interviews, 2012, 2013.

8. James Wood, telephone interview, 2012.

9. Frank Vega, personal interviews, 2012, 2013. Numerous other accounts on file about RAAF personnel who were immediately transferred after incident, including outside personnel from Fort Worth, White Sands, Wright Field, and Fitzsimmons with special assignment to Roswell at the time of the incident.

10. Ibid.

11. All quotes from this paragraph from James Wood, telephone interview, 2012.

12. Ibid.

13. Ibid.

14. Ibid.

Chapter 10

1. Geraldine Perkins, personal interview, 2000.

2. All in this paragraph from Cordy Derek, telephone interviews, 2008.

3. All here from Jo Ann Purdie, telephone interviews, 2008.

4. Joe Brazel, personal interviews, 2002–2015.

5. Bill Brazel, personal interviews, 1989–2003.

6. Shirley Brazel, personal interviews, 1989–1996.

7. Sally Tadolini, telepohone interviews, 1989. This demonstrates a wonderful example of creating a visualization of Tadolini's

immediate impression of the unknown material and how she related it specifically to a common occurrence she participated in: the act of ironing clothes—no wrinkles.

8. Bill Brazel, personal interviews, 1989–2003.

9. All in this paragraph from Fawn Fritz, personal interviews, 2003–2015.

10. Charles A. McGee, Major USAFR, telephone interviews, 1992–1993.

11. Ibid.

12. Walter Haut, personal interview, 1998. The interview was a result of a comment he made in 1998 to Milton C. Sprouse, who was a Staff Sergeant with the 830th Bomb Squadron stationed at the RAAF in 1947.

13. All here from Steven Akins, personal interview and telephone interviews, 1990. Akins was able to demonstrate to us with a topographical map the approximate location to which he transported the two unknown officers. It was the general area of the Brazel debris field.

14. Recollection and quotations from James Parker, personal interview, 1990. As has long been the policy of the present owners of the former Foster ranch where Mack Brazel originally discovered the debris field, we too have maintained a professional agreement as to not publicly divulge the location or ever mention the name of the owner. Ranch hand Parker was no exception as he was never informed about any details of the 1947 incident, until after his experience with the Air Force trespassers in 1987.

Chapter 11

1. *Newsweek*, September 1994.

2. Biography of William Randolph Lovelace II, New Mexico Museum of Space History, International Space Hall of Fame.

3. McAndrew, James, *The Roswell Report, Case Closed,* Headquarters U.S. Air Force: U.S. Government Printing Office, 1997.
4. Ibid.
5. Samuel Alderson, Biography, *Encyclopedia Britannica.*
6. Jeremy Alderson, Phone interview, email correspondence, 2013.
7. Ibid.
8. Ibid (all quotes in paragraph).
9. Biography of William Randolph Lovelace II.
10. Ibid.
11. Mark D. Erasmus, personal interview, 2011.
12. June Crain, telephone interviews, 1993. In *The Truth About the UFO Crash at Roswell* (Randle and Schmitt, 1994), we identified Crain by the pseudonym Sarah Holcomb at her request. Nevertheless, her testimony has always been totally consistent. NOTE: For a full account of June Crain, the authors highly recommend *Tell My Story; June Crain, The Air Force & UFOs* by James E. Clarkson.
13. Ibid.

Chapter 12

1. Tom Brookshier, telephone interview conducted by Tom Carey, July 2008.
2. Lyon, Bill, "'Brookie' Unpretentious, Fun, a Friend to All," *For the Inquirer,* posted on *philly.com, www.philly.com/philly/sports/eagles/20100131_Bill_Lyon_ Brookie_ upretentious,* January 31, 2010.
3. Plati, David. "Football, Broadcasting Legend Tom Brookshier Passes Away," *CUBuffs.com,* January 30, 2010.
4. Wilkinson, Gerry, and Ed Harvey, "Tom Brookshier," Broadcast Pioneers of Philadelphia, *www.broadcastpioneers.com/tombrookshier.html.* January 18, 2006, with an Addendum added to original article in 2010 after Brookshier's death.

5. Note the different spelling of young Brookshier's first name. It was derived from a picture of his youth baseball team that appeared in the *Roswell Daily Record* the last week of June 1947, with his first name spelled "Tommie" instead of "Tom" or "Tommy."

6. Tom Brookshier, telephone interview conducted by Tom Carey, July 2008.

7. Wilkinson and Harvey, "Tom Brookshier."

8. Story details and quotations in this paragraph from Tom Brookshier, telephone interview conducted by Tom Carey, July 2008.

9. Jo Tyner, telephone interview, January 2008.

10. Tom Brookshier, telephone interview conducted by Tom Carey, July 2008.

11. Monkovic, Toni, "Remembering Tom Brookshier," *The Fifth Down—The New York Times N.F.L. Blog*, January 31, 2010.

12. Tom Brookshier, telephone interview conducted by Tom Carey, July 2008.

13. *NFL Game of the Week*, watched by Tom Carey; teams and date unknown. NOTE: The mysterious object in the sky was not mentioned in the press reports of the game, but it still remains as an "unknown" in Carey's memory.

Chapter 13

1. Juanita Kaufmann, personal interviews, 1990–2002.

2. Randle and Schmitt, *UFO Crash at Roswell*.

3. Frank Kaufmann, personal interviews, 1990–2001.

4. Ibid.

5. Ibid. Down to a man, every officer or soldier we have interviewed who has provided testimony as to the central location of all activity concerning the incident has pointed

to Hangar P-3, today known as Building 84. It should be no surprise that given the preponderance of testimony that the base was under "lockdown" during that same period, specific areas would have been designated as "off limits" such as the very building where the wreckage and remains were being stored until transit. It should also be no surprise that Kaufmann would have been aware of such restrictions and occasionally supplied us with corroborative data.

6. Congressional Recognition of Goddard Rocket and Space Museum Roswell, New Mexico, U.S. government, Washington, DC: May 28, 1970. "Frank Kaufmann, Executive Vice President of the Roswell Chamber of Commerce, has through the years, made a notable contribution. National leaders such as Dr. von Braun and Dr. Gilruth have taken time from busy schedules to participate in important dedications of the Goddard Rocket and Space Museum," p. 37. Kaufmann repeatedly claimed that his association with von Braun was in connection with the 1947 incident.

7. Meeting with *CBS 48 Hours* producer at CUFOS office, Chicago, Ill., 1994.

8. Statement from CBS correspondent Phil Jones after our first dinner meeting.

9. *"UFOs, Alien Cover-Ups; Roswell—Pt. 4, CBS 48 Hours*, April 1995.

10. The source here is a telephone conversation with a CBS producer who asked to remain anonymous, 1995, in which the producer stated that they had conducted a "thorough" investigation of Kaufmann's background and concluded that "he was who he said he was."

11. Edward G. Modell, personal interview, 1994.

12. Max Littell, personal interviews, 1990–2000.

13. *UFO Crash at Roswell: An Audio Documentary*, 1997, Baraka Foundation.

14. Philip J. Corso, personal interview, 1997.

15. Arne Oldman, personal interviews, 1998; and Steven Johnson, personal interviews, 1998.

16. Frank Kaufmann, personal interviews, 1990–2001. When Don Schmitt originally was shown the impact site north of Roswell in 1993 by Kaufmann, they went approximately 10 miles past the correct turnoff. After turning back to what Kaufmann claimed was the correct road, they proceeded on for 3 miles off Highway 285. Upon returning to Roswell, Kaufmann later called and then claimed that they needed to go 2 more miles beyond the earlier site. Over the next two years, Kaufmann would relent and suggest that the "true" location was "10 miles further north."

17. Frank Kaufmann, personal interviews, 1990–2001. From the first time we were introduced to Captain "Edwards," as described by Kaufmann, leading up to this writing of this book, this figure still remains an enigma. Still, just prior to his death, according to his family, some Air Force officer paid him one final visit. Unfortunately for us, the chances of establishing who he is or, more importantly, if he ever existed, is at a dead end.

18. The Franklin Mint Roswell Incident UFO Witness Sculpture, C Licensed by Worth Point, Hallmarked 1997. Based on witness Frank J. Kaufmann.

19. William McDonald, forensic artist, provided technical illustrations for the ship based on Kaufmann's own sketches to Testors in 1995, whereas Shadowbox Company used the Kaufmann alien illustration from *The Truth About the UFO Crash at Roswell* drawn by Don Schmitt in 1998.

20. Kaufmann had three handcrafted replicas of his ship design presented to him. Don Schmitt has the one given to him by Kaufmann, which was originally made for him by artist Terry R. Erlewine in 1997.

21. Rick Kaufmann, personal interviews, 2000–2001.

22. Ibid.

23. Julie Shuster, personal interviews, 2000–2001.

24. Jack Rodden, personal interviews, 2000–2001.

25. Juanita Kaufmann, personal interviews, 1990–2002; Rick Kaufmann, personal interviews, 2000–2001.

26. Juanita Kaufmann, personal interviews, 1990–2002; Jack Rodden, personal interviews, 2000–2001; and Julie Shuster, personal interviews, 2000–2001.

27. Juanita Kaufmann, personal interviews, 1990–2002.

28. Mark Rodeghier and Mark Chesney made a gentlemen's agreement with Don Schmitt not to publicly divulge any of the newly found negative information concerning Frank Kaufmann until the passing of his widow, Juanita. It was not until the Fall 2002 issue of *The International Reporter (IUR), Volume 27, Number 3*, that the article "Frank Kaufmann Reconsidered" was published, officially breaking the story.

29. William J. Birnes, personal interview, 2007.

30. Paul Davids, executive producer of *ROSWELL*, is the son of Jules Davids, the co-author of the John F. Kennedy Pulitzer Prize–winning book *Profiles in Courage*. Davids was a professor of diplomatic history at Georgetown University in Washington, DC. One of his students was Jacqueline Kennedy—and after that, Bill Clinton, who did his undergraduate work there. Paul and his wife, Hollace, were invited to Clinton's 1992 presidential inauguration. In 1993 Davids personally presented President Clinton with an autographed copy of *UFO Crash at Roswell* by Randle and Schmitt, and in 2008 a copy of *Witness to Roswell* by Carey and Schmitt.

31. Frank Kaufmann, personal interviews, 1990–2001.

32. Ibid.

33. Mike Fischer, executive manager, Roswell Chamber of Commerce, 2002.

34. Private briefing of Stanton T. Friedman by Don Schmitt, July 2001.

35. The surreal oil painting with the face of one of Kaufmann's aliens was fully examined by Don Schmitt immediately following the death of Juanita Kaufmann in 2002, in the presence of the surviving grandchildren. The stretched canvas painting was thoroughly inspected for the possible final hiding place of some physical evidence or documentation. Nothing was present, though it was observed that the alien was not the original work, as it was a more recent painting over a previous work on the same canvas.

36. Frank Kaufmann, personal interviews, 1990–2001.

Chapter 14

1. Both quotes in this paragraph from *Roswell Daily Record*, July 9, 1947.

2. Loretta Proctor, personal Interviews, 1989–2009.

3. Ibid.

4. Ibid.

5. U.S. Navy History, USS Hassayampa.

6. Fawn Fritz, personal interviews, 2002 – 2015.

7. Bill Brazel, personal interviews, 1989–2003.

8. James Schreiber, personal interview, 2003.

9. Bill Brazel, personal interviews, 1989–2003.

10. Mark Wolf, former TV news anchor, CNN, Rochester, N.Y. Producer, director, and producer of *UFO Secret; The Roswell Crash*. 1991. Freedom of Information Request; Records Search, Santa Fe, New Mexico, 2001.

11. Both quotes here from Bill Brazel, personal interviews, 1989–2003.

12. Berlitz and Moore, *The Roswell Incident.*

13. *UFOs—What's Going On?* Home Box Office, 1985. Produced, directed, and written by Directors Guild of America Award winner Robert Guenetto. Guenetto was the president of the International Documentary Association.

14. Recollection and quotations from Brazel Schrieber, personal interview, 2004; and Bessie Brazel Schrieber, personal interview, 2003.

15. Bill Brazel, personal interview, 2003; and Bessie Schrieber, personal interview, 2003.

16. Geraldine Perkins, personal interview, 2003.

17. Loretta Proctor, telephone interview, 2003.

18. Joe and Beverly Brazel, personal interview, 2003.

Bibliography

Balint, Ed. "Canton's Close Encounter," in *The Repository,* August 22, 2010.

Berlitz, Charles, and William L. Moore. *The Roswell Incident* (New York: Grosset & Dunlap, 1980).

Carey, Thomas J., and Donald R. Schmitt. *Witness to Roswell* (Franklin Lakes/Pompton Plains, N.J.: The Career Press/New Page Books, 2007, 2009).

Congressional Recognition of Goddard Rocket and Space Museum, Roswell, New Mexico. Washington, D.C.: U.S. government, May 28, 1970.

Duggar, Barbara. Videotaped interview in *Recollections of Roswell, Part II* (Mt. Rainier, Md.: Fund for UFO Research, Inc., 1992).

"Frank Kaufmann Reconsidered." *The International UFO Reporter, Vol. 27, No. 3* (Chicago, Ill.: The Center for UFO Studies, 2002).

"General Ramey Empties Roswell Saucer." *Roswell Daily Record,* July 9, 1947.

Goldstein, Richard. "Tom Brookshier, Eagles Star and Broadcaster, Dies at 78." *The New York Times,* January 31, 2010, *www. nytimes.com/2010/01/31/sports/football/31brookshier. html?ref=obituaries.*

Grant, Taylor. *ABC Nightly News.* July 8 and July 9, 1947.

Guenetto, Robert. *UFOs—What's Going On?* (Los Angeles, Calif.: Home Box Office Special Presentation, 1985).

"Harassed Rancher Who Located 'Saucer' Sorry He Told About It." *Roswell Daily Record,* July 9, 1947.

Kromschroeder, John. Videotaped interview in *Recollections of Roswell, Part II* (Mt. Rainier, Md.: Fund for UFO Research, Inc., 1992).

Marcel, Jesse, Jr., and Linda Marcel. *The Roswell Legacy: The Untold Story of the First Military Officer at the 1947 Crash Site* (Franklin Lakes, N.J.: The Career Press/New Page Books, 2009).

McGuire, Phyllis. Videotaped interview in *Recollections of Roswell, Part II* (Mt. Rainier, Md.: Fund for UFO Research, Inc., 1992).

Monkovic, Toni. "Remembering Tom Brookshier." *The Fifth Down—The New York Times NFL Blog,* January 31, 2010.

Multer-Lingle, Sundi, personal interviews conducted by William E. Jones and Irina McCammon, in *Ohio UFO Notebook* (Columbus, Ohio: 1994).

"RAAF Captures Flying Saucer on Ranch in Roswell Region." *Roswell Daily Record,* July 8, 1947.

Randle, Kevin D., and Donald R. Schmitt. *UFO Crash at Roswell* (New York: Avon Books, 1991).

Roswell [New Mexico] City Directory, 1947.

"Sheriff Wilcox Takes Leading Role in Excitement Over Report 'Saucer' Found." *Roswell Daily Record,* July 9, 1947.

"Sports People; [Tom] Brookshier Penalized." *The New York Times,* December 14, 1983, *www.nytimes.com/1983/12/14/sports/ sports-people-brookshier-penalized.html.*

Tulk, Elizabeth. Videotaped interview in *Recollections of Roswell, Part II* (Mt. Rainier, Md.: Fund for UFO Research, Inc., 1992).

U.S. Navy History: USS HASSAYAMPA (Washington, D.C.: U.S. government, Naval Records Division, 1988).

Wilkinson, Gerry, and Ed Harvey. "Tom Brookshier," *Broadcast Pioneers of Philadelphia,* January 18, 2006, *www. broadcastpioneers.com/tombrookshier.html.* Addendum added to original 2010 article after Brookshier's death.

Wolf, Mark. *UFO Secret: The Roswell Crash* video (Poway, Calif.: New Century Productions, 1993).

Index

About the Authors

Thomas J. Carey, a native Philadelphian, holds degrees from Temple University (BS in business administration) and California State University, Sacramento (MA in anthropology), and also attended the University of Toronto's PhD Programme in Anthropology. An Air Force veteran who held a TOP SECRET/CRYPTO clearance, Tom is now a retired Philadelphia area businessman. He was a Mutual UFO Network (MUFON) State Section Director for Southeastern Pennsylvania from 1986 to 2001, a Special Investigator for the J. Allen Hynek Center for UFO Studies (CUFOS) from 1991 to 2001, and a member of the CUFOS board of directors from 1997 to 2001. Tom began investigating aspects of the Roswell Incident in 1991 for the Roswell investigative team of Kevin Randle and Don Schmitt, and since 1998 has teamed exclusively with Don Schmitt to continue a *proactive* investigation of the case. Tom has authored or co-authored more than 40 published articles about the Roswell events of 1947, and has contributed to a number of books on the subject. He has appeared as a guest on many radio and TV shows throughout the country, including *Coast to Coast AM* with Art Bell and George Noory, *Fox and Friends, Comcast Network Friends,* and *Larry King Live!,* and has contributed to a number of Roswell-related documentaries, on-screen and behind the scenes. Tom was a consultant and interviewee on the highly acclaimed and rated 2002, two-hour SyFy Channel documentary, *The Roswell Crash:*

Startling New Evidence; the History Channel's *Conspiracy Theory*; the Travel Channel's *Weird Travels—Roswell*; the SyFy Channel's *SyFy Investigates*; and the History Channel's *The UFO Hunters*. He was also a featured interviewee on the 20th Century Fox, golden anniversary re-release DVD of the 1951 sci-fi classic, *The Day the Earth Stood Still*. His 2007 book, co-authored with Don Schmitt, *Witness to Roswell: Unmasking the 60-Year Cover-Up*, was the number-one best-selling UFO book in the world in 2007–2008. Its sequel, *Witness to Roswell: Unmasking the Government's Biggest Cover-Up* (2009), remains a best-seller. Both books are considered to be the best books ever written about the "Roswell Incident." A motion picture based upon these books titled *Majic Men* is planned, as is a TV mini-series. A recent book about the secret history of Wright-Patterson Air Force Base in Dayton, Ohio, titled *Inside the Real Area 51*, also co-authored with Don Schmitt (2013), reached number one in Amazon's Astronomy & Space Science category and was also in its Top 100 Books of the Year in that category for 2013. A final Roswell book, *Roswell: The Verdict of History*, is planned for a 2017 release, the 70th anniversary year of the incident. Tom and his wife, Doreen, have two grown children and reside in Huntingdon Valley, Pennsylvania.

Donald R. Schmitt is the former Director of Special Investigations for the J. Allen Hynek Center for UFO Studies (CUFOS) in Chicago, where he also served on the board of directors for 10 years. He is a co-founder of the International UFO Museum and Research Center (IUFOMRC) in Roswell and serves as an advisor to the Board of Directors. A five-time best-selling author, his first book, co-authored with Dr. Kevin D. Randle, *UFO Crash at Roswell*, was made into the Golden Globe–nominated, made-for-TV movie *Roswell*.

His recent book, *Witness to Roswell*, co-authored with Thomas J. Carey, was the number-one selling UFO book in the world for 2007 and 2008. The book has been optioned for feature-film production by Stellar Productions under the title *Majic Men*. He is also an associate producer of the upcoming feature film *701*, scripted by Peabody Award–winning writer Tracy Torme.

A renowned international speaker in such countries as Japan, Australia, Brazil, Mexico, Europe, and the United Kingdom, Don has appeared on *Oprah*, *CBS 48 Hours*, *Larry King Live*, *ABC News*, *NBC News*, *CNN*, *Paul Harvey News*, and hundreds more programs. A graduate of Concordia University, *cum laude*, he resides in Holy Hill, Wisconsin, with his wife, Marie.